Hamilton Beach Indoor Grill Cookbook 1000

300 Easy Tasty Recipes for Your Hamilton Beach Electric Indoor Searing Grill (Less Smoke and Easy to Operate)

By Kalinda Jenson

TABLE OF CONTENTS

CHAPTER 4: VEGAN & VEGEATARIAN RECIPES

CHAPTER 5: APPETIZERS AND SIDE DISHES

v

Introduction

Hello, friend! Welcome to the Hamilton Beach Indoor Grill Cookbook!

This is cookbook is for Hamilton Beach Indoor Grill cooking, which will guide you to be a professional indoor Barbecuer and Griller! Before we dive into the recipes, let's know about the essentials of this appliance!

Hamilton Beach Indoor Grill makes healthy grilling at home a breeze. Temperature setting, dishwasher safe plates & drip tray. Adjustable temperature control ranges from 200 degree to high searing temperature of 450 degree.

Hamilton Beach 25361 Indoor Grill

Enjoy perfectly grilled meats and veggies any time of year with the Hamilton Beach Searing Grill. No longer do you have to fire up the outdoor grill to cook a couple of steaks or wait until winter is over to enjoy a juicy grilled burger. With a high searing temperature that locks in juices and an adjustable temperature knob to customize grilling, you're sure to have delicious results every time.

The Hamilton Beach Searing Grill is easy to use. Indicator lights let you know when your grill is on and ready for use. The lid window lets you watch your food as it cooks and the large, non-stick, cooking surface allows enough space to grill multiple items at once. It also comes with an extra-large drip tray to catch excess juice or grease.

Convenient grilling is only part of what makes this product perfect for your busy lifestyle. It is also simple to clean. Both the grill surface and the drip tray are removable and dishwasher safe. In addition, the grill cover can also be removed for hand washing. With the Hamilton Beach Searing Grill you can enjoy restaurant quality meats on the grill all year long ...now that's Good Thinking.

- Window lets you watch food as it cooks
- Removable nonstick plate and drip tray for easy dishwasher cleanup
- Get outdoor flavor... indoors - high searing temperature locks in juices and flavor
- Adjustable temperature control and power and preheat lights
- Removable lid for easy cleanup

Get outdoor flavors indoors

The Hamilton Beach Searing Grill's high-heat searing temperature locks in juices and flavor, giving your meat better taste, texture and appearance. After searing, the adjustable temperature control lets you complete the cooking process without worrying about overcooking from heat that is too high. Much like your outdoor grill, your meat will cook to perfection under the grills unique hooded design that helps to keep flavor in and gives your food that authentic outdoor grilled taste.

Removable Grill Plate

The grill plate is removable for easy cleaning. It is even dishwasher safe.

No Mess
The drip pan is large enough to capture any juices that escape. It easily slides out for cleaning.

Cover Slides Off
The outdoor grill style dome lid is perfect for locking in flavors, but it too can get a bit messy at times. Luckily it was designed to be removable so that it can be washed when needed.

Searing Perfection
Cooking with the Searing Grill is easy. Simply turn the temperature dial all

the way up to sear. When it reaches the high searing temperature of 450 degrees, the green preheat light will glow. Now you're ready to sear steaks, burgers, pork chops or fish fillets to perfection. If you want to grill food that doesn't need to sear first, use the adjustable temperature dial to grill at a lower heat.

Hamilton Beach Indoor Grills
Restaurant-quality results don't have to come from a steakhouse. Instead, they start at home with an indoor grill that does what most grills can't: keep meat tender and juicy without overcooking it.

Hamilton Beach Indoor Grills have what it takes to bring out meat's best flavor. And since our indoor grills are built with ease in mind, you also get convenient features such as electronic controls, indicator lights, and removable grids that go in the dishwasher.

Now let's dig in the recipes!

Chapter 1: Red Meat Recipes

Smoked and pulled beef

Prep time: 10 minutes, Cook time: 6 hours; Serves: 6

Ingredients

- 4 lb beef sirloin tip roast
- 1/2 cup bbq rub
- 2 bottles of amber beer
- 1 bottle barbecues sauce

Preparation Method

1. Coat the steak with bbq rub and let it smoke on the grill for 1 hour.
2. Continue cooking and flipping the steak for the next 3 hours. Transfer the steak to a braising vessel .add the beers.
3. Braise the beef until tender then transfer to a platter reserving 2 cups of cooking liquid.
4. Use a pair of forks to shred the beef and return it to the pan. Add the reserved liquid and barbecue sauce. Stir well and keep warm before serving.
5. Enjoy.

Smoked Beef Jerky

Prep time: 15 minutes, Cook time: 5 hours; Serves: 10

Ingredients

- 3 lb sirloin steaks, sliced into 1/4 inch thickness
- 2 cups soy sauce
- 1/2 cup brown sugar
- 1 cup pineapple juice
- 2 tbsp sriracha

- 2 tbsp red pepper flake
- 2 tbsp hoisin
- 2 tbsp onion powder
- 2 tbsp rice wine vinegar
- 2 tbsp garlic, minced

Preparation Method

1. Mix all the ingredients in a ziplock bag. Seal the bag and mix until the beef is well coated. Ensure you get as much air as possible from the ziplock bag.
2. Put the bag in the fridge overnight to let marinate. Remove the bag from the fridge 1 hour prior to cooking.
3. Let them cook for 5 hours while turning after every 2-1/2 hours.
4. Transfer from the grill and let cool for 30 minutes before serving.
5. enjoy.

Reverse Seared Flank Steak

Prep time: 10 minutes, Cook time: 10 minutes; Serves: 2

Ingredients

- 1.5 lb Flanks steak
- 1 tbsp salt
- 1/2 onion powder
- 1/4 tbsp garlic powder
- 1/2 black pepper, coarsely ground

Preparation Method

1. Preheat your grill to 225°F.
2. In a mixing bowl, mix salt, onion powder, garlic powder, and pepper. Generously rub the steak with the mixture.
3. Place the steaks on the preheated grill and let the steak cook.

mixed.

2. Trim any excess fat from the meat and slice into 1/4 inch slices. Add the steak with the marinade into a zip lock bag and let marinate for 12-24 hours in a fridge.
3. Set the grill to smoke and let preheat for 5 minutes.
4. Arrange the steaks on the grill leaving a space between each. Let smoke for 5 hours.
5. Remove the steak from grill and serve when warm.

Grilled Butter Basted Rib-eye

Prep time: 20 minutes, Cook time: 20 minutes; Serves: 4

Ingredients

- 2 rib-eye steaks, bone-in
- Slat to taste
- Pepper to taste
- 4 tbsp butter, unsalted

Preparation Method

1. Mix steak, salt, and pepper in a ziplock bag. Seal the bag and mix until the beef is well coated. Ensure you get as much air as possible from the ziplock bag.
2. Set the grill temperature to high with closed lid for 15 minutes. Place a cast-iron into the grill.
3. Place the steaks on the hottest spot of the grill and cook for 5 minutes with the lid closed.
4. Open the lid and add butter to the skillet. When it's almost melted place the steak on the skillet with the grilled side up.
5. Cook for 5 minutes while busting the meat with butter. Close the lid and cook until the internal temperature is 130°F.
6. Remove the steak from skillet and let

rest for 10 minutes before enjoying with the reserved butter.

Smoked Brisket

Prep time: 20 minutes, Cook time: 9 hours; Serves: 10

Ingredients

- 2 tbsp garlic powder
- 2 tbsp onion powder
- 2 tbsp paprika
- 2 tbsp chili powder
- 1/3 cup salt
- 1/3 cup black pepper
- 12 lb whole packer brisket, trimmed
- 1-1/2 cup beef broth

Preparation Method

1. Set your Grill temperature to 225°F. Let preheat for 15 minutes with the lid closed.
2. Meanwhile, mix garlic, onion, paprika, chili, salt, and pepper in a mixing bowl.
3. Season the brisket generously on all sides.
4. Place the meat on the grill with the fat side down and let it cool until the internal temperature reaches 160°F.
5. Remove the meat from the grill and double wrap it with foil. Return it to the grill and cook until the internal temperature reaches 204°F.
6. Remove from grill, unwrap the brisket and let est for 15 minutes.
7. Slice and serve.

Smoked Ribeye Steaks

Prep time: 15 minutes, Cook time: 35 minutes; Serves: 1

Ingredients

- 2-inch thick ribeye steaks
- Steak rub of choice

Preparation Method

1. Preheat your Grill to low smoke.
2. Sprinkle the steak with your favorite steak rub and place it on the grill. Let it smoke for 25 minutes.
3. Remove the steak from the grill and set the temperature to 400°F.
4. Return the steak to the grill and sear it for 5 minutes on each side.
5. Cook until the desired temperature is achieved; 125°F-rare, 145°F-Medium, and 165°F.-Well done.
6. Wrap the steak with foil and let rest for 10 minutes before serving. Enjoy.

Nutritional Information

Calories 225, Total fat 10.4g, Saturated fat 3.6g, Total Carbs 0.2g, Net Carbs 0.2g, Protein 32.5g, Sugar 0g, Fiber 0g, Sodium: 63mg, Potassium 463mg

Smoked Trip tip with java Chophouse

Prep time: 10 minutes, Cook time: 90 minutes; Serves: 4

Ingredients

- 2 tbsp olive oil
- 2 tbsp java chophouse seasoning
- 3 lb trip tip roast, fat cap and silver skin removed

Preparation Method

1. Startup your grill and smoker and set the temperature to 225°F.
2. Rub the roast with olive oil and seasoning then place it on the smoker rack.
3. Smoke until the internal temperature is 140°F.
4. Remove the tri-tip from the smoker and let rest for 10 minutes before serving. Enjoy.

Supper Beef Roast

Prep time: 5 minutes, Cook time: 3 hours; Serves: 7

Ingredients

- 3-1/2 beef top round
- 3 tbsp vegetable oil
- Prime rib rub
- 2 cups beef broth
- 1 russet potato, peeled and sliced
- 2 carrots, peeled and sliced
- 2 celery stalks, chopped
- 1 onion, sliced
- 2 thyme sprigs

Preparation Method

1. Rub the roast with vegetable oil and place it on the roasting fat side up. Season with prime rib rub then pour the beef broth.
2. Set the temperature to 500°F and preheat the grill for 15 minutes with the lid closed.
3. Cook for 30 minutes or until the roast is well seared.
4. Reduce temperature to 225°F. Add the veggies and thyme and cover with foil. Cook for 3 more hours o until the internal temperature reaches 135°F.
5. Remove from the grill and let rest for 10 minutes. Slice against the grain and serve with vegetables and the pan dippings.
6. Enjoy.

grill Deli-style Roast beef

Prep time: 15 minutes, Cook time: 4 hours; Serves: 2

Ingredients

- 4lb round-bottomed roast
- 1 tbsp coconut oil

- 1/4 tbsp garlic powder
- 1/4 tbsp onion powder
- 1/4 tbsp thyme
- 1/4 tbsp oregano
- 1/2 tbsp paprika
- 1/2 tbsp salt
- 1/2 tbsp black pepper

Preparation Method

1. Combine all the dry hubs to get a dry rub.
2. Roll the roast in oil then coat with the rub.
3. Set your grill to 185°F and place the roast on the grill.
4. Smoke for 4 hours or until the internal temperature reaches 140°F.
5. Remove the roast from the grill and let rest for 10 minutes.
6. Slice thinly and serve.

Simple Smoked Pork ribs

Prep time: 15 minutes, Cook time: 5 hours; Serves: 7

Ingredients

- 3 rack baby back ribs
- 3/4 cup pork and poultry rub
- 3/4 cup Que BBQ Sauce

Preparation Method

1. Peel the membrane from the backside of the ribs and trim any fat.
2. Season the pork generously with the rub.
3. Set the grill to 180°F and preheat for 15 minutes with the lid closed.
4. Place the pork ribs on the grill and smoke them for 5 hours.
5. Remove the pork from the grill and wrap them in a foil with the BBQ sauce.
6. Place back the pork and increase the temperature to 350°F. Cook for 45 more minutes.
7. Remove the pork from the grill and let it rest for 20 minutes before serving. Enjoy.

Roasted Pork with Balsamic Strawberry Sauce

Prep time: 15 minutes, Cook time: 35 minutes; Serves: 3

Ingredients

- 2 lb pork tenderloin
- Salt and pepper to taste
- 2 tbsp rosemary, dried
- 2 tbsp olive oil
- 12 strawberries, fresh
- 1 cup balsamic vinegar
- 4 tbsp sugar

Preparation Method

1. Set the grill to 350°F and preheat for 15 minutes with a closed lid.
2. Meanwhile, rinse the pork and pat it dry. Season with salt, pepper, and rosemary.
3. In an oven skillet, heat oil until smoking. Add the pork and sear on all sides until golden brown.
4. Set the skillet in the grill and cook for 20 minutes or until the meat is no longer pink and the internal temperature is 150°F.
5. Remove the pork from the grill and let rest for 10 minutes.
6. Add berries to the skillet and sear over the stovetop for a minute. Remove the strawberries from the skillet.
7. Add vinegar in the same skillet and scrape any browned bits from the skillet bottom. Bring it to boil then reduce heat to low. Stir in sugar and cook until it has reduced by half.
8. Slice the meat and place the strawberries on top then drizzle vinegar sauce. Enjoy.

grill pork crown Roast

Prep time: 5 minutes, Cook time: 1 hour;
Serves: 5

Ingredients

- 13 ribs pork
- 1/4 cup favorite rub
- 1 cup apple juice
- 1 cup Apricot BBQ sauce

Preparation Method

1. Set the Grill temperature to 375°F to preheat for 15 minutes with the lid closed.
2. Meanwhile, season the pork with the rub then let sit for 30 minutes.
3. Wrap the tips of each crown roast with foil to prevent the borns from turning black.
4. Place the meat on the grill grate and cook for 90 minutes. Spray apple juice every 30 minutes.
5. When the meat has reached an internal temperature of 125°F remove the foils.
6. Spray the roast with apple juice again and let cook until the internal temperature has reached 135°F.
7. In the last 10 minutes of cooking, baste the roast with BBQ sauce.
8. Remove from the grill and wrap with foil. Let rest for 15 minutes before serving. Enjoy.

Wet-Rubbed St. Louis Ribs

Prep time: 15 minutes, Cook time: 4 hours;
Serves: 3

Ingredients

- 1/2 cup brown sugar
- 1 tbsp cumin, ground
- 1 tbsp Ancho Chile powder
- 1 tbsp smoked paprika
- 1 tbsp garlic salt
- 3 tbsp balsamic vinegar
- 1 Rack St. Louis style ribs
- 2 cup apple juice

Preparation Method

1. Add all the ingredients except ribs in a mixing bowl and mix until well mixed. Place the rub on both sides of the ribs and let sit for 10 minutes.
2. Set the Grill temperature to 180°F and preheat for 15 minutes. Smoke the ribs for 2 hours.
3. Increase the temperature to 250°F and wrap the ribs and apple juice with foil or in tinfoil.
4. Place back the pork and cook for an additional 2 hours.
5. Remove from the grill and let rest for 10 minutes before serving. Enjoy.

Cocoa Crusted Pork Tenderloin

Prep time: 30 minutes, Cook time: 25 minutes; Serves: 5

Ingredients

- 1 pork tenderloin
- 1/2 tbsp fennel, ground
- 2 tbsp cocoa powder, unsweetened
- 1 tbsp smoked paprika
- 1/2 tbsp kosher salt
- 1/2 tbsp black pepper
- 1 tbsp extra virgin olive oil
- 3 green onion

Preparation Method

1. Remove the silver skin and the connective tissues from the pork loin.
2. Combine the rest of the ingredients in a mixing bowl, then rub the mixture on the pork. Refrigerate for 30 minutes.
3. Preheat the grill for 15 minutes with the lid closed.

4. Sear all sides of the loin at the front of the grill then reduce the temperature to 350°F and move the pork to the centre grill.
5. Cook for 15 more minutes or until the internal temperature is 145°F.
6. Remove from grill and let rest for 10 minutes before slicing. Enjoy

grilled Bacon

Prep time: 30 minutes, Cook time: 25 minutes; Serves: 6

Ingredients

- 1 lb. bacon, thickly cut

Preparation Method

1. Preheat your grill to 375°F.
2. Line a baking sheet with parchment paper then place the bacon on it in a single layer.
3. Close the lid and bake for 20 minutes. Flip over, close the lid, and bake for an additional 5 minutes.
4. Serve with the favorite side and enjoy.

grilled pork Chops

Prep time: 20 minutes, Cook time: 10 minutes; Serves: 6

Ingredients

- 6 pork chops, thickly cut
- BBQ rub

Preparation Method

1. Preheat the Grill to 450°F.
2. Season the pork chops generously with the bbq rub. Place the pork chops on the grill and cook for 6 minutes or until the internal temperature reaches 145°F.
3. Remove from the grill and let sit for 10 minutes before serving.
4. Enjoy.

Blackened Pork Chops

Prep time: 5 minutes, Cook time: 20 minutes; Serves: 6

Ingredients

- 6 pork chops
- 1/4 cup blackening seasoning
- Salt and pepper to taste

Preparation Method

1. Preheat your grill to 375°F.
2. Meanwhile, generously season the pork chops with the blackening seasoning, salt, and pepper.
3. Place the pork chops on the grill and close the lid.
4. Let grill for 8 minutes then flip the chops. Cook until the internal temperature reaches 142°F.
5. Remove the chops from the grill and let rest for 10 minutes before slicing.
6. Serve and enjoy.

Grilled Tenderloin with fresh herb sauce

Prep time: 10 minutes, Cook time: 15 minutes; Serves: 4

Ingredients

Pork
- 1 pork tenderloin, silver skin removed and dried
- BBQ seasoning

Fresh herb sauce
- 1 handful basil, fresh
- 1/4 tbsp garlic powder
- 1/3 cup olive oil
- 1/2 tbsp kosher salt

Preparation Method

1. Preheat the grill to medium heat.
2. Coat the pork with BBQ seasoning then cook on semi-direct heat of the grill.

Turn the pork regularly to ensure even cooking.
3. Cook until the internal temperature is 145°F. Remove from the grill and let it rest for 10 minutes.
4. Meanwhile, make the herb sauce by pulsing all the sauce ingredients in a food processor. Pulse for a few times or until well chopped.
5. Slice the pork diagonally and spoon the sauce on top. Serve and enjoy.

grilled shredded pork tacos

Prep time: 15 minutes, Cook time: 7 hours; Serves: 8

Ingredients

- 5 lb pork shoulder, bone-in

Dry Rub

- 3 tbsp brown sugar
- 1 tbsp salt
- 1 tbsp garlic powder
- 1 tbsp paprika
- 1 tbsp onion powder
- 1/4 tbsp cumin
- 1 tbsp cayenne pepper

Preparation Method

1. Mix all the dry rub ingredients and rub on the pork shoulder.
2. Preheat the grill to 275°F and cook the pork directly for 6 hours or until the internal temperature has reached 145°F.
3. If you want to fall off the bone tender pork, then cook until the internal temperature is 190°F.
4. Let rest for 10 minutes before serving. Enjoy

Togarashi Pork tenderloin

Prep time: 5 minutes, Cook time: 25 minutes; Serves: 6

Ingredients

- 1 Pork tenderloin
- 1/2tbsp kosher salt
- 1/4 cup Togarashi seasoning

Preparation Method

1. Cut any excess silver skin from the pork and sprinkle with salt to taste. Rub generously with the togarashi seasoning
2. Place in a preheated oven at 400°F for 25 minutes or until the internal temperature reaches 145°F.
3. Remove from the grill and let rest for 10 minutes before slicing and serving.
4. Enjoy.

Nutritional Information

Calories 390, Total fat 13g, Saturated fat 6g, Total Carbs 4g, Net Carbs 1g, Protein 33g, Sugar 0g, Fiber 3g, Sodium: 66mg

Pulled Pork

Prep time: 15 minutes, Cook time: 12 hours; Serves: 12

Ingredients

- 8 lb pork shoulder roast, bone-in
- BBQ rub
- 3 cups apple cider, dry hard

Preparation Method

1. Fire up the grill and set it to smoke.
2. Meanwhile, rub the pork with bbq rub on all sides then place it on the grill grates. cook for 5 hours, flipping it every 1 hour.
3. Increase the heat to 225°F and continue cooking for 3 hours directly on the grate.
4. Transfer the pork to a foil pan and place the apple cider at the bottom of the pan.
5. Cook until the internal temperature reaches 200°F then remove it from the grill. Wrap the pork loosely with foil then let it rest for 1 hour.

6. Remove the fat layer and use forks to shred it.
7. Serve and enjoy.

Smoked Pork Ribs

Prep time: 15minutes, Cook time: 10 hours; Serves: 4

Ingredients

- 2 racks baby back ribs
- 1 cup homemade BBQ rub
- 24 oz hard apple cider
- 1 cup dark brown sugar
- 2 batches homemade BBQ sauce

Preparation Method

1. Set your Grill to smoke.
2. Remove the membrane from the pork ribs then generously coat with bbq sauce.
3. Smoke at 175°F for 5 hours. Increase the grill temperature to 225°F.
4. Transfer the pork to a high sided pan that has been sprayed with cooking spray.
5. Pour over the apple cider and rub the pork with sugar. Cover the pan with foil and place it back to the grill. Cook for 4 more hours.
6. Transfer the ribs from the pan to the grill grate and increase the temperature to 300°F.
7. Brush the ribs with BBQ sauce 3 times in the next 1 hour. Remove the ribs from the grill and serve them. Enjoy.

Smoked Spicy Candied Bacon

Prep time: 5 minutes, Cook time: 35 minutes; Serves: 6

Ingredients

- 1 lb centre cut bacon
- 1/2 cup dark brown sugar

- 1/2 cup maple syrup
- 1 tbsp sriracha hot sauce
- 1/2 tbsp cayenne pepper

Preparation Method

1. In a mixing bowl, combine sugar, maple syrup, sriracha sauce, and cayenne pepper.
2. Preheat the grill to 300°F.
3. Line a baking pan with parchment paper and lay the bacon on it in a single layer. Brush the bacon with the sugar mixture until well coated.
4. Place the baking pan in the grill and cook for 20 minutes. Flip the bacon and cook for 15 more minutes.
5. Remove the bacon from the grill and let cool for 10 minutes before removing from the baking pan and serving.
6. Enjoy.

Smoked Lamb Shoulder

Prep time: 10 minutes, Cook time: 1hour 30 minutes; Serves: 7

Ingredients

For Smoked Lamb Shoulder
- 5 lb lamb shoulder, boneless and excess fat trimmed
- 2 tbsp kosher salt
- 2 tbsp black pepper
- 1 tbsp rosemary, dried

The Injection
- 1 cup apple cider vinegar

The Spritz
- 1 cup apple cider vinegar
- 1 cup apple juice

Preparation Method

1. Preheat the smoker with a water pan to 225°F.
2. Rinse the lamb in cold water then pat it dry with a paper towel. Inject vinegar to

the lamb.

3. Pat the lamb dry again and rub with oil, salt black pepper and rosemary. Tie with kitchen twine.
4. Smoke uncovered for 1 hour then spritz after every 15 minutes until the internal temperature reaches 195^0 F.
5. Remove the lamb from the grill and place it on a platter. Let cool before shredding it and enjoying it with your favorite side.

Smoked Pulled Lamb Sliders

Prep time: 10 minutes, Cook time: 7 hours; Serves: 7

Ingredients

For the Lamb's shoulder
- 5 lb lamb shoulder, boneless
- 1/2 cup olive oil
- 1/4 cup dry rub
- 10 oz spritz

The Dry Rub
- 1/3 cup kosher salt
- 1/3 cup pepper, ground
- 1-1/3 cup garlic, granulated

The Spritz
- 4 oz Worcestershire sauce
- 6 oz apple cider vinegar

Preparation Method

1. Preheat the smoker with a water bath to 250^0 F.
2. Trim any fat from the lamb then rub with oil and dry rub.
3. Place the lamb on the smoker for 90 minutes then spritz with a spray bottle every 30 minutes until the internal temperature reaches 165^0 F.
4. Transfer the lamb shoulder to a foil pan with the remaining spritz liquid and cover tightly with foil.
5. Place back in the smoker and smoke

until the internal temperature reaches 200^0 F.
6. Remove from the smoker and let rest for 30 minutes before pulling the lamb and serving with slaw, bun, or aioli. Enjoy

Crown rack of lamb

Prep time: 10 minutes, Cook time: 30 minutes; Serves: 6

Ingredients
- 2 racks of lamb, frenched
- 1 tbsp garlic, crushed
- 1 tbsp rosemary, finely chopped
- 1/4 cup olive oil
- 2 feet twine

Preparation Method

1. Rinse the racks with cold water then pat them dry with a paper towel.
2. Lay the racks on a flat board then score between each bone, about 1/4 inch down.
3. In a mixing bowl, mix garlic, rosemary, and oil then generously brush on the lamb.
4. Take each lamb rack and bend it into a semicircle forming a crown-like shape.
5. Use the twine to wrap the racks about 4 times starting from the base to the top. Make sure you tie the twine tightly to keep the racks together.
6. Preheat the Smoker to 400-450^0 F then place the lamb racks on a baking dish. Plac ethe baing dish on the Grill.
7. Cook for 10 minutes then reduce temperature to 300^0 F. cook for 20 more minutes or until the internal temperature reaches 130^0 F.
8. Remove the lamb rack from the Smoker and let rest for 15 minutes.
9. Serve when hot with veggies and

potatoes. Enjoy.

Smoked Leg of Lamb

Prep time: 15 minutes, Cook time: 3hourss; Serves: 6

Ingredients

- 1 leg lamb, boneless
- 4 garlic cloves, minced
- 2 tbsp salt
- 1 tbsp black pepper, freshly ground
- 2 tbsp oregano
- 1 tbsp thyme
- 2 tbsp olive oil

Preparation Method

1. Trim any excess fat from the lamb and tie the lamb using twine to form a nice roast.
2. In a mixing bowl, mix garlic, spices, and oil. Rub all over the lamb, wrap with a plastic bag then refrigerate for an hour to marinate.
3. Place the lamb on a smoker set at 250^0 F. smoke the lamb for 4 hours or until the internal temperature reaches 145^0 F.
4. Remove from the smoker and let rest to cool. Serve and enjoy.

grilled Aussie Leg of Lamb Roast

Prep time: 30 minutes, Cook time: 2 hours; Serves: 8

Ingredients

- 5 lb Aussie leg of lamb, boneless

Smoked Paprika Rub

- 1 tbsp raw sugar
- 1 tbsp kosher salt
- 1 tbsp black pepper
- 1 tbsp smoked paprika
- 1 tbsp garlic powder
- 1 tbsp rosemary, dried
- 1 tbsp onion powder

- 1tbsp cumin
- 1/2 tbsp cayenne pepper

Roasted Carrots

- 1 bunch rainbow carrots
- Olive oil
- Salt
- pepper

Preparation Method

1. Heat the grill to 375^0 F.
2. Trim any excess fat from the lamb.
3. Combine all the rub ingredients and rub all over the lamb. Place the lamb on the grill and smoke for 2 hours.
4. Toss the carrots in oil, salt, and pepper then add to the grill after the lamb has cooked for 1-1/2 hour.
5. Cook until the roast internal temperature reaches 135^0 F. Remove the lamb from the grill and cover with foil. Let rest for 30 minutes.
6. Remove the carrots from the grill once soft and serve with the lamb. Enjoy.

Simple Grilled Lamb Chops

Prep time: 10 minutes, Cook time: 6 minutes; Serves: 6

Ingredients

- 1/4 cup distilled white vinegar
- 2 tbsp salt
- 1/2 tbsp black pepper
- 1 tbsp garlic, minced
- 1 onion, thinly sliced
- 2 tbsp olive oil
- 2lb lamb chops

Preparation Method

1. In a resealable bag, mix vinegar, salt, black pepper, garlic, sliced onion, and oil until all salt has dissolved.
2. Add the lamb chops and toss until well coated. Place in the fridge to marinate

for 2 hours.

3. Preheat the grill to high heat.
4. Remove the lamb from the fridge and discard the marinade. Wrap any exposed bones with foil.
5. Grill the lamb for 3 minutes per side. You can also broil in a broiler for more crispness. Serve and enjoy

grilled Lamb with Brown Sugar Glaze

Prep time: 15 minutes, Cook time: 10 minutes; Serves: 4

Ingredients

- 1/4 cup brown sugar
- 2 tbsp ginger, ground
- 2 tbsp tarragon, dried
- 1 tbs cinnamon, ground
- 1 tbsp black pepper, ground
- 1 tbsp garlic powder
- 1/2 tbsp salt
- 4 lamb chops

Preparation Method

1. In a mixing bowl, mix sugar, ginger, dried tarragon, cinnamon, black pepper, garlic, and salt.
2. Rub the lamb chops with the seasoning and place it on a plate.refrigerate for an hour to marinate.
3. Preheat the grill to high heat then brush the grill grate with oil.
4. Arrange the lamb chops on the grill grate in a single layer and cook for 5 minutes on each side.
5. Serve and enjoy.

Grilled leg of lambs Steaks

Prep time: 10 minutes, Cook time: 10 minutes; Serves: 4

Ingredients

- 4 lamb steaks, bone-in
- 1/4 cup olive oil
- 4 garlic cloves, minced
- 1 tbsp rosemary, freshly chopped
- Salt and black pepper

Preparation Method

1. Place the lamb in a shallow dish in a single layer. Top with oil, garlic cloves, rosemary, salt, and black pepper then flip the steaks to cover on both sides.
2. Let sit for 30 minutes to marinate.
3. Preheat the grill to high and brush the grill grate with oil.
4. Place the lamb steaks on the grill grate and cook until browned and the internal is slightly pink. The internal temperature should be 140^0 F.
5. Let rest for 5 minutes before serving. Enjoy.

grilled Lamb Loin Chops

Prep time: 10 minutes, Cook time: 10 minutes; Serves: 6

Ingredients

- 2 tbsp herbs de Provence
- 1-1/2 tbsp olive oil
- 2 garlic cloves, minced
- 2 tbsp lemon juice
- 5 oz lamb loin chops
- Salt and black pepper to taste

Preparation Method

1. In a small mixing bowl, mix herbs de Provence, oil, garlic, and juice. Rub the mixture on the lamb chops then refrigerate for an hour.
2. Preheat the grill to medium-high then lightly oil the grill grate.
3. Season the lamb chops with salt and black pepper.

4. Place the lamb chops on the grill and cook for 4 minutes on each side.
5. Remove the chops from the grill and place them in an aluminum covered plate. Let rest for 5 minutes before serving. Enjoy.

Spicy Chinese Cumin Lamb Skewers

Prep time: 20 minutes, Cook time: 6 minutes; Serves: 10

Ingredients

- 1lb lamb shoulder, cut into 1/2 inch pieces
- 10 skewers
- 2 tbsp ground cumin
- 2 tbsp red pepper flakes
- 1 tbsp salt

Preparation Method

1. Thread the lamb pieces onto skewers.
2. Preheat the grill to medium heat and lightly oil the grill grate.
3. Place the skewers on the grill grate and cook while turning occasionally. Sprinkle cumin, pepper flakes, and salt every time you turn the skewer.
4. Cook for 6 minutes or until nicely browned. Serve and enjoy.

grill Dale's Lamb

Prep time: 15 minutes, Cook time: 50 minutes; Serves: 8

Ingredients

- 2/3 cup lemon juice
- 1/2 cup brown sugar
- 1/4 cup Dijon mustard
- 1/4 cup soy sauce
- 1/4 cup olive oil
- 2 garlic cloves, minced

- 1 piece ginger root, freshly sliced
- 1 tbsp salt
- 1/2 tbsp black pepper, ground
- 5 lb leg of lamb, butterflied

Preparation Method

1. In a mixing bowl, mix lemon juice, sugar, dijon mustard, sauce, oil, garlic cloves, ginger root, salt, and pepper.
2. Place the lamb in a dish and pour the seasoning mixture over it. Cover the dish and put in a fridge to marinate for 8 hours.
3. Preheat a grill to medium heat. Drain the marinade from the dish and bring it to boil in a small saucepan.
4. Reduce heat and let simmer while whisking occasionally.
5. Oil the grill grate and place the lamb on it. Cook for 50 minutes or until the internal temperature reaches 145^0 F while turning occasionally.
6. Slice the lamb and cover with the marinade. Serve and enjoy.

Garlic and Rosemary Grilled Lamb Chops

Prep time: 10 minutes, Cook time: 20 minutes; Serves: 4

Ingredients

- 2 lb lamb loin, thick-cut
- 4 garlic cloves, minced
- 1 tbsp kosher salt
- 1/2 tbsp black pepper
- 1 lemon zest
- 1/4 cup olive oil

Preparation Method

1. In a small mixing bowl, mix garlic, lemon zest, oil, salt, and black pepper then pour the mixture over the lamb.

18

2. Flip the lamb chops to make sure they are evenly coated. Place the chops in the fridge to marinate for an hour.
3. Preheat the grill to high heat then sear the lamb for 3 minutes on each side.
4. Reduce the heat and cook the chops for 6 minutes or until the internal temperature reaches 150^0 F.
5. Remove the lamb from the grill and wrap it in a foil. Let it rest for 5 minutes before serving. Enjoy.

Grilled LambChops

Prep time: 1 hour, Cook time: 8 minutes; Serves: 3

Ingredients

- 2 garlic cloves, crushed
- 1 tbsp rosemary leaves, fresh chopped
- 2 tbsp olive oil
- 1 tbsp lemon juice, fresh
- 1 tbsp thyme leaves, fresh
- 1 tbsp salt
- 9 lamb loin chops

Preparation Method

1. Add the garlic, rosemary, oil, juice, salt, and thyme in a food processor. Pulse until smooth.
2. Rub the marinade on the lamb chops both sides and let marinate for 1 hour in a fridge. Remove from the fridge and let sit at room temperature for 20 minutes before cooking.
3. Preheat your Smokerto high heat. smoke the lamb chops for 5 minutes on each side.
4. Sear the lamb chops for 3 minutes on each side. Remove from the grill and serve with a green salad.

Grilled Beef Jerky

Prep time: 15 minutes, Cook time: 5 hours; Serves 10

Ingredients

- 3 lb sirloin steaks
- 2 cups soy sauce
- 1 cup pineapple juice
- 1/2 cup brown sugar
- 2 tbsp sriracha
- 2 tbsp hoisin
- 2 tbsp red pepper flake
- 2 tbsp rice wine vinegar
- 2 tbsp onion powder

Preparation Method

1. Mix the marinade in a zip lock bag and add the beef. Mix until well coated and remove as much air as possible.
2. Place the bag in a fridge and let marinate overnight or for 6 hours. Remove the bag from the fridge an hour prior to cooking
3. Startup the Grill and set it on the smoking settings or at 190^0F.
4. Lay the meat on the grill leaving a half-inch space between the pieces. Let cool for 5 hours and turn after 2 hours.
5. Remove from the grill and let cool. Serve or refrigerate

Smoked Beef Roast

Prep time: 10 minutes, Cook time: 6 hours; Serves 6

Ingredients

- 1-3/4 lb beef sirloin tip roast
- 1/2 cup bbq rub
- 2 bottles amber beer
- 1 bottle BBQ sauce

Preparation Method

1. Turn the Grill onto the smoke setting.
2. Rub the beef with bbq rub until well coated then place on the grill. Let smoke

for 4 hours while flipping every 1 hour.
3. Transfer the beef to a pan and add the beer. The beef should be 1/2 way covered.
4. Braise the beef until fork tender. It will take 3 hours on the stovetop and 60 minutes on the instant pot.
5. Remove the beef from the ban and reserve 1 cup of the cooking liquid.
6. Use 2 forks to shred the beef into small pieces then return to the pan with the reserved braising liquid.
7. Add BBQ sauce and stir well then keep warm until serving. You can also reheat if it gets cold.

Reverse Seared Flank Steak

Prep time: 10 minutes, Cook time: 20 minutes; Serves 2 steaks

Ingredients

- 3 lb flank steaks
- 1 tbsp salt
- 1/2 tbsp onion powder
- 1/4 tbsp garlic powder
- 1/2 black pepper, coarsely ground

Preparation Method

1. Preheat the Grill to 225^0F.
2. All the ingredients in a bowl and mix well. Add the steaks and rub them generously with the rub mixture.
3. Place the steak on the grill and close the lid. Let cook until its internal temperature is 10^0F under your desired temperature. 115^0F for rare, 125^0F for the medium rear and 135^0F for medium.
4. Wrap the steak with foil and raise the grill temperature to high. Place back the steak and grill for 3 minutes on each side.
5. Pat with butter and serve when hot.

Grilled Beef Tenderloin

Prep time: 10 minutes, Cook time: 45 minutes; Serves 6

Ingredients

- 4 lb beef tenderloin
- 3 tbsp steak rub
- 1 tbsp kosher salt

Preparation Method

1. Preheat the Grill to high heat.
2. Meanwhile, trim excess fat from the beef and cut it into 3 pieces.
3. Coat the steak with rub and kosher salt. Place it on the grill.
4. Close the lid and cook for 10 minutes. Open the lid, flip the beef and cook for 10 more minutes.
5. Reduce the temperature of the grill until 225^0F and smoke the beef until the internal temperature reaches 130^0F.
6. Remove the beef from the grill and let rest for 15 minutes before slicing and serving.

Grilled New York Strip

Prep time: 5 minutes, Cook time: 15 minutes; Serves 6

Ingredients

- 3 New York strips
- Salt and pepper

Preparation Method

1. If the steak is in the fridge, remove it 30 minutes prior to cooking.
2. Preheat the Grill to 450^0F.
3. Meanwhile, season the steak generously with salt and pepper. Place it on the grill and let it cook for 5 minutes per side or until the internal temperature reaches 128^0F.
4. Remove the steak from the grill and let it rest for 10 minutes.

Grilled Stuffed Peppers

Prep time: 20 minutes, Cook time: 5 minutes; Serves 6

Ingredients

- 3 bell peppers, sliced in halves
- 1 lb ground beef, lean
- 1 onion, chopped
- 1/2 tbsp red pepper flakes
- 1/2 tbsp salt
- 1/4 tbsp pepper
- 1/2 tbsp garlic powder
- 1/2 tbsp onion powder
- 1/2 cup white rice
- 15 oz stewed tomatoes
- 8 oz tomato sauce
- 6 cups cabbage, shredded
- 1-1/2 cup water
- 2 cups cheddar cheese

Preparation Method

1. Arrange the pepper halves on a baking tray and set aside.
2. Preheat your grill to 325°F.
3. Brown the meat in a large skillet. Add onions, pepper flakes, salt, pepper garlic, and onion and cook until the meat is well cooked.
4. Add rice, stewed tomatoes, tomato sauce, cabbage, and water. Cover and simmer until the rice is well cooked, the cabbage is tender and there is no water in the rice.
5. Place the cooked beef mixture in the pepper halves and top with cheese.
6. Place in the grill and cook for 30 minutes.
7. Serve immediately and enjoy it.

Grilled Prime Rib Roast

Prep time: 10 minutes, Cook time: 2 hours; Serves 8

Ingredients

- 5 lb rib roast, boneless
- 4 tbsp salt
- 1 tbsp black pepper
- 1-1/2 tbsp onion powder
- 1 tbsp granulated garlic
- 1 tbsp rosemary
- 1 cup chopped onion
- 1/2 cup carrots, chopped
- 1/2 cup celery, chopped
- 2 cups beef broth

Preparation Method

1. Remove the beef from the fridge 1 hour prior to cooking.
2. Preheat the Grill to 250°F.
3. In a small mixing bowl, mix salt, pepper, onion, garlic, and rosemary to create your rub.
4. Generously coat the roast with the rub and set it aside.
5. Combine chopped onions, carrots, and celery in a cake pan then place the bee on top.
6. Place the cake pan in the middle of the Grill and cook for 1 hour.
7. Pour the beef broth at the bottom of the cake pan and cook until the internal temperature reaches 120°F.
8. Remove the cake pan from the Grill and let rest for 20 minutes before slicing the meat.
9. Pour the cooking juice through a strainer, then skim off any fat at the top.
10. Serve the roast with the cooking juices.

Grilled Kalbi Beef short Ribs

Prep time: 10 minutes, Cook time: 6 hours; Serves 6

Ingredients

- 1/2 cup soy sauce

- 1/2 cup brown sugar
- 1/8 cup rice wine
- 2 tbsp minced garlic
- 1 tbsp sesame oil
- 1/8 cup onion, finely grated
- 2-1/2 lb beef short ribs, thinly sliced

Preparation Method

1. Mix soy sauce, sugar, rice wine, garlic, sesame oil and onion in a medium mixing bowl.
2. Add the beef in the bowl and cover it in the marinade. Cover the bowl with a plastic wrap and refrigerate for 6 hours.
3. Heat your Grill to high and ensure the grill is well heated.
4. Place the marinated meat on the grill and close the lid ensuring you don't lose any heat.
5. Cook for 4 minutes, flip, and cook for 4 more minutes on the other side.
6. Remove the meat and serve with rice and veggies of choice. Enjoy.

Grilled Beef Short Rib Lollipop

Prep time: 15 minutes, Cook time: 3 hours; Serves 4

Ingredients
- 4 beef short rib lollipops
- BBQ Rub
- BBQ Sauce

Preparation Method

1. Preheat your Grill to 275^{0}F.
2. Season the short ribs with BBQ rub and place them on the grill.
3. Cook for 4 hours while turning occasionally until the meat is tender.
4. Apply the sauce on the meat in the last 30 minutes of cooking.
5. Serve and enjoy.

Grilled Tri-Tip

Prep time: 10 minutes, Cook time: 1 hour 30 minutes; Serves 6

Ingredients
- 3 lb tri-tip
- 1-1/2 tbsp kosher salt
- 1 tbsp black pepper
- 1 tbsp paprika
- 1/2 tbsp cayenne
- 1 tbsp onion powder
- 1 tbsp garlic powder

Preparation Method

1. Preheat your Grill to 250^{0}F.
2. Mix the seasoning ingredients and generously season the tri-tip.
3. Place it in the Grill and cook for 30 minutes. Flip the tri-tip and cook for an additional 30 minutes.
4. Turn up the Grill and coo for additional 30 minutes. Pull out the meat at 125^{0}F for medium-rare and 135^{0}F for medium.
5. Let the meat rest for 10 minutes before slicing and serving.

Grilled Smoked Lamb Chops

Prep time: 10 minutes, Cook time: 50 minutes; Serves 4

Ingredients
- 1 rack lamb
- 2 tbsp rosemary, fresh
- 2 tbsp sage, fresh
- 1 tbsp thyme, fresh
- 2 garlic cloves, roughly chopped
- 2 tbsp shallots, roughly chopped
- 1/2 tbsp salt
- 1/2 tbsp ground pepper
- 1/4 cup olive oil
- 1 tbsp honey

Preparation Method

1. Preheat the Grill to 225^{0}F

2. Trim any excess fat and silver skin from the lamb.
3. Combine the rest of the ingredients in the food processor and generously rub the lamb with the seasoning.
4. Place the seasoned lamb on the Grill and cook for 45 minutes or until the internal temperature reaches 120^0F.
5. Sear the lamb on the Grill for 2 minutes per side or until the internal temperature reaches 125^0F for medium-rare or 145^0F for medium.
6. Let rest for 5 minutes before slicing it. Enjoy

Grilled Smoked Lamb Shoulder

Prep time: 20 minutes, Cook time: 3 hours; Serves 7

Ingredients

- 5 lb. lamb shoulder
- 1 cup cider vinegar
- 2 tbsp. oil
- 2 tbsp. kosher salt
- 2 tbsp. black pepper, freshly ground
- 1 tbsp. dried rosemary

For the Spritz

- 1 cup apple cider vinegar
- 1 cup apple juice

Preparation Method

1. Preheat the Grill to 225^0F with a pan of water for moisture.
2. Trim any excess fat from the lamb and rinse the meat in cold water. Pat dry with a paper towel.
3. Inject the cider vinegar in the meat then pat dry with a clean paper towel.
4. Rub the meat with oil, salt, black pepper, and dried rosemary. Tie the lamb shoulder with a twine.
5. Place in the smoker for an hour then

spritz after every 15 minutes until the internal temperature reaches 165^0F.
6. Remove from the Grill and let rest for 1 hour before shredding and serving.

Smoked Pulled Lamb Sliders

Prep time: 10 minutes, Cook time: 9 hours; Serves 7

Ingredients

- 5 lb. lamb shoulder, boneless
- 1/2 cup olive oil
- 1/3 cup kosher salt
- 1/3 cup pepper, coarsely ground
- 1/3 cup granulated garlic

For the spritz

- 4 oz Worcestershire sauce
- 6 oz apple cider vinegar

Preparation Method

1. Preheat the Grill to 225^0F with a pan of water for moisture.
2. Trim any excess fat from the lamb then pat it dry with some paper towel. Rub with oil, salt, pepper, and garlic.
3. Place the lamb in the Smoker for 90 minutes then spritz every 30 minutes until the internal temperature reaches 165^0F.
4. Transfer the lamb in a foil pan then add the remaining spritz liquid. Cover with a foil and place back in the Grill.
5. Smoke until the internal temperature reaches 205^0F.
6. Remove from the smoker and let rest in a cooler without ice for 30 minutes before pulling it.
7. Serve with slaw or bun and enjoy.

Smoked Lamb Meatballs

Prep time: 10 minutes, Cook time: 1 hour; Serves 20 meatballs

Ingredients

- 1 lb. lamb shoulder, ground
- 3 garlic cloves, finely diced
- 3 tbsp. shallot, diced
- 1 tbsp. salt
- 1 egg
- 1/2 tbsp. pepper
- 1/2 tbsp. cumin
- 1/2 tbsp. smoked paprika
- 1/4 tbsp. red pepper flakes
- 1/4 tbsp. cinnamon
- 1/4 cup panko breadcrumbs

Preparation Method

1. Set your Grill to 250^0F .
2. Combine all the ingredients in a small bowl then mix thoroughly using your hands.
3. Form golf ball-sized meatballs and place them in a baking sheet.
4. Place the baking sheet in the smoker and smoke until the internal temperature reaches 160^0F.
5. Remove the meatballs from the smoker and serve when hot.

Grilled Crown Rack Of Lamb

Prep time: 30 minutes, Cook time: 30 minutes; Serves 6

Ingredients

- 2 racks of lamb. Frenched
- 1 tbsp garlic, crushed
- 1 tbsp rosemary
- 1/2 cup olive oil
- Kitchen twine

Preparation Method

1. Preheat your Grill to 450^0F.
2. Rinse the lab with clean cold water then pat it dry with a paper towel.
3. Lay the lamb flat on a chopping board and score a ¼ inch down between the bones. Repeat the process between the bones on each lamb rack. Set aside.
4. In a small mixing bowl, combine garlic, rosemary, and oil. Brush the lamb of rack generously with the mixture.
5. Bend the lamb rack into a semicircle then place the racks together such that the bones will be up and will form a crown shape.
6. Wrap around 4 times starting from the base moving upward. Tie tightly to keep the racks together.
7. Place the lambs on a baking sheet and set in the Grill. Cook on high heat for 10 minutes. Reduce the temperature to 300^0F and cook for 20 more minutes or until the internal temperature reaches 130^0F.
8. Remove the lamb rack from the Grill and let rest while wrapped in a foil for 15 minutes.
9. Serve when hot.

Smoked Leg

Prep time: 15 minutes, Cook time: 3 hours; Serves 6

Ingredients

- 1 leg of lamb, boneless
- 2 tbsp oil
- 4 garlic cloves, minced
- 2 tbsp oregano
- 1 tbsp thyme
- 2 tbsp salt
- 1 tbsp black pepper, freshly ground

Preparation Method

1. Trim excess fat from the lamb ensuring you keep the meat in an even thickness for even cooking.
2. In a mixing bowl, mix oil, garlic, and all spices. Rub the mixture all over the lamb then cover with a plastic wrap.

3. Place the lamb in a fridge and let marinate for an hour.
4. Transfer the lamb on a smoker rack and set the Grill to smoke at 250^{0}F.
5. Smoke the meat for 4 hours or until the internal temperature reaches 145^{0}F.
6. Remove from the Grill and serve immediately.

Grilled Aussie Leg of Lamb

Prep time: 30 minutes, Cook time: 2 hours; Serves 8

Ingredients

- 5 lb Aussie Boneless Leg of lamb

Smoked Paprika Rub

- 1 tbsp raw sugar
- 1 tbsp salt
- 1 tbsp black pepper
- 1 tbsp smoked paprika
- 1 tbsp garlic powder
- 1 tbsp rosemary
- 1 tbsp onion powder
- 1 tbsp cumin
- 1/2 tbsp cayenne pepper

Roasted Carrots

- 1 bunch rainbow carrots
- Olive oil
- Salt and pepper

Preparation Method

1. Preheat your Grill to 350^{0}F and trim any excess fat from the meat.
2. Combine the paprika rub ingredients and generously rub all over the meat.
3. Place the lamb on the preheated Grill over indirect heat and smoke for 2 hours.
4. Meanwhile, toss the carrots in oil, salt, and pepper.
5. Add the carrots to the grill after 1 ½ hour or until the internal temperature has reached 90^{0}F.
6. Cook until the meat internal temperature reaches 135^{0}F.
7. Remove the lamb from the Grill and cover it with foil for 30 minutes.
8. Once the carrots are cooked serve with the meat and enjoy.

Simple Grilled Lamb Chops

Prep time: 10 minutes, Cook time: 20 minutes; Serves 6

Ingredients

- 1/4 cup white vinegar, distilled
- 2 tbsp olive oil
- 2 tbsp salt
- 1/2 tbsp black pepper
- 1 tbsp minced garlic
- 1 onion, thinly sliced
- 2 lb lamb chops

Preparation Method

1. In a resealable bag, mix vinegar, oil, salt, black pepper, garlic, and sliced onions until all salt has dissolved.
2. Add the lamb and toss until evenly coated. Place in a fridge to marinate for 2 hours.
3. Preheat your Grill.
4. Remove the lamb from the resealable bag and leave any onion that is stuck on the meat. Use an aluminum foil to cover any exposed bone ends.
5. Grill until the desired doneness is achieved. Serve and enjoy when hot.

Grilled Lamb with Sugar Glaze

Prep time: 15 minutes, Cook time: 20 minutes; Serves 4

Ingredients

- 1/4 cup sugar

- 2 tbsp ground ginger
- 2 tbsp dried tarragon
- 1/2 tbsp salt
- 1 tbsp black pepper, ground
- 1 tbsp ground cinnamon
- 1 tbsp garlic powder
- 4 lamb chops

Preparation Method

1. In a mixing bowl, mix sugar, ground ginger, tarragon, salt, pepper, cinnamon, and garlic.
2. Rub the lamb chops with the mixture and refrigerate for an hour.
3. Meanwhile, preheat your Grill.
4. Brush the grill grates with oil and place the marinated lamb chops on it. Cook for 5 minutes on each side.
5. Serve and enjoy.

Nutritional Information

Calories 241, Total fat 13.1g, Saturated fat 5.6g, Total carbs 15.8g, Net carbs 15.1g Protein 14.6g, Sugars 13.6g, Fiber 0.7g, Sodium 339.2mg, Potassium 256.7mg

Grilled Leg of Lamb Steak

Prep time: 10 minutes, Cook time: 10 minutes; Serves 4

Ingredients

- 4 eaches lamb steaks, bone-in
- 1/4 cup olive oil
- 4 garlic cloves, minced
- 1 tbsp rosemary, freshly chopped
- Salt and pepper to taste

Preparation Method

1. Arrange the steak in a dish in a single layer. Cover the meat with oil, garlic, fresh rosemary, salt, and pepper.
2. Flip the meat to coat on all sides and let it marinate. For 30 minutes.

3. Preheat your Grill and lightly oil the grates cook the meat on the grill until well browned on both sides and the internal temperature reaches 140^0F.
4. Serve and enjoy.

Grilled Pork Chops

Prep time: 15 minutes, Cook time: 20 minutes; Serves 6

Ingredients

- 6 thick-cut pork chops
- BBQ rub

Preparation Method

1. Preheat your Grill to 450^0F.
2. Season the pork chops with the BBQ rub.
3. Place the chops on the Grill and cook for 6 minutes on each side or until the internal temperature reaches 145^0F.
4. Remove the chops from the Grill and let cool for 5 minutes before serving.

Grilled Bacon

Prep time: 5 minutes, Cook time: 25 minutes; Serves 6

Ingredients

- 1lb bacon

Preparation Method

1. Preheat your Grill to 375^0F.
2. Line a baking sheet with parchment paper then arrange the thick-cut bacon on it in a single layer.
3. Bake the bacon in the Grill for 20 minutes. Flip the bacon pieces and cook for 20 more minutes or until the bacon is no longer floppy. Serve and enjoy.

Grilled Blackened Pork Chops

Prep time: 5 minutes, Cook time: 20 minutes; Serves 6

Ingredients

- 6 pork chops
- 1/4 cup blackening seasoning
- Salt and pepper

Preparation Method

1. Preheat your Grill to 375^{0}F.
2. Generously season the pork chops with the blackening seasoning, salt, and pepper.
3. Place the chops on the Grill and cook for 8 minutes on one side then flip.
4. Cook until the internal temperature reaches 142^{0}F.
5. Let the pork chops rest for 10 minutes before slicing and serving.

Grilled Teriyaki Pineapple Pork Tenderloin Sliders

Prep time: 30 minutes, Cook time: 2 hours; Serves 6

Ingredients

- 1-1/2 lb. pork tenderloin
- 1 can pineapple rings
- 1 pack Kings Hawaiian rolls
- 8 oz. teriyaki sauce
- 1-1/2 tbsp. salt
- 1 tbsp. onion powder
- 1 tbsp. paprika
- 1/2 tbsp. garlic powder
- 1/2 tbsp. cayenne pepper

Preparation Method

1. Preheat your Grill to 325^{0}F.
2. Add all the rub ingredients and evenly apply on the pork tenderloin.
3. Place the pork on the preheated Grill and cook while turning every 4 minutes. Cook until the internal temperature of the meat is 145^{0}F.
4. Meanwhile, place the pineapple rings on the grill and cook them until nicely browned.
5. As the pineapples are cooking cut the Hawaiin rolls into halves and place them on the grill until toasty brown.
6. Remove the pork from the Grill and let rest for 5 minutes.
7. Assemble the sliders by put a bottom roll, followed by pork tenderloin, pineapple ring, some teriyaki sauce, and the top roll.
8. enjoy

Grilled Pork Tenderloin with Herb sauce

Prep time: 10 minutes, Cook time: 15 minutes; Serves 4

Ingredients

- 1 pork tenderloin
- Bbq seasoning

Fresh Herb Sauce

- 1 handful basil, fresh
- 1/2 handful flat-leaf parsley, fresh
- 1/4 tbsp garlic powder
- 1/3 cup olive oil
- 1/2 tbsp kosher salt

Preparation Method

1. Preheat your Grill to medium heat.
2. Remove silver skin from the pork tenderloin and pat it dry with a paper towel.
3. Generously rub the pork with the bbq seasoning then cook over indirect heat in the Grill while turning occasionally.
4. Cook until the internal temperature reaches 145^{0}F. Remove the pork from the Grill and let rest for 10 minutes.
5. Meanwhile, add all the fresh herb sauce ingredients in a food processor and pulse a few times.

6. Slice the pork tenderloin diagonally and spoon the sauce on top. Serve

Grilled Shredded Pork Tacos

Prep time: 15 minutes, Cook time: 7 hours; Serves 8

Ingredients

- 5 lb pork shoulder, bone-in

Dry Rub

- 3 tbsp. brown sugar
- 1 tbsp. salt
- 1 tbsp. garlic powder
- 1 tbsp. paprika
- 1 tbsp. onion powder
- 1/4 tbsp. cumin
- 1 tbsp. cayenne pepper

Preparation Method

1. Combine the dry rub ingredients in a mixing bowl then rub the pork roast.
2. Place the pork on the Grill at 250^{0}F at indirect heat for 7 hours or until the internal temperature reaches 145^{0}F.
3. Remove the pork from the Grill and let rest for 10 minutes before shredding.
4. Serve with tacos and enjoy

Grilled Togarashi Pork Tenderloin

Prep time: 5 minutes, Cook time: 25 minutes; Serves 4

Ingredients

- 1 pork tenderloin
- 1/2 tbsp. kosher salt
- 1/4 cup Togarashi seasoning

Preparation Method

1. Trim off any silver skin on the pork tenderloin then sprinkle salt and togarashi seasoning evenly.

2. Preheat the Grill to 400^{0}F.
3. Cook the pork for 25 minutes or until the internal temperature reaches 145^{0}F.
4. Remove the pork from the Grill and let rest for 10 minutes before slicing and serving.

Grilled pulled pork

Prep time: 15 minutes, Cook time: 12 hours; Serves 12

Ingredients

- 8 lb. pork shoulder roast, bone-in
- BBQ Rub
- 3 cups dry hard apple cider vinegar

Preparation Method

1. Fire up your Grill and set it at the smoke setting.
2. Rub the pork shoulder with the BBQ rub then place it on the grill grates. Smoke for 5 hours while turning it every hour.
3. Increase the heat o 225^{0}F and continue cooking for to 3 more hours.
4. Transfer the pork roast to a foil pan with apple cider vinegar at the bottom.
5. Continue cooking the roast until it reaches an internal temperature of 200^{0}F.
6. Remove the pork from the Grill and remove the skin and any fat layer from the meat. shred it using 2 forks and serve

Smoked Pork Ribs

Prep time: 15 minutes, Cook time: 10 hours; Serves 4

Ingredients

- 2 racks back ribs
- 1 cup homemade bbq rub
- 2 12-oz hard apple cider

- 1 cup dark brown sugar
- 2 batches homemade BBQ sauce

Preparation Method

1. Turn the Grill to smoke setting and remove any membrane from the meat.
2. Place the pork in the Grill and smoke for 5 hours or until it reaches an internal temperature of 175.
3. Increase the grill temperature to 225^0F. Transfer the meat to a pan sprayed with cooking spray.
4. Pour one bottle of hard apple cider to the pan and rub the brown sugar on top of the ribs.
5. Cover the pan with tin foil and place it back to the Grill. Cook for 4 hours.
6. Remove the tin foil, increase the temperature to 300^0F, and place the ribs on the grill grates.
7. Cook for 1 hour brushing the ribs with BBQ sauce 3 times.
8. The ribs should now be falling off the bone. Let rest for 5 minutes before serving.

Smoked Spicy Candied Bacon

Prep time: 5 minutes, Cook time: 35 minutes; Serves 6

Ingredients

- 1 lb. center cut bacon
- 1/2 cup dark brown sugar
- 1/2 cup real maple syrup
- 1 tbsp sriracha hot sauce
- 1/2 tbsp. cayenne pepper

Preparation Method

1. In a small mixing bowl, whisk together sugar, maple syrup, hot sauce, and cayenne until well combined.
2. Preheat your Grill to 300^0F and line a baking sheet with parchment paper.

3. Lay the bacon on a single layer and brush with the sugar mixture on both sides.
4. Place the baking sheet in the Grill and cook for 20 minutes. Flip the bacon and cook for 15 more minutes.
5. Remove the baking sheet from the Grill and let cool for 15 minutes before serving.

Cool Brisket

Prep Time: 20 minutes/ Cook Time 3 hours 30 minutes/ Serves: 4

Ingredients:

- Apple cider vinegar
- 2 teaspoons cayenne pepper
- 2 tablespoons ground coriander
- 2 tablespoons oregano
- 2 tablespoons onion powder
- 4 tablespoons ground cumin
- 4 tablespoons black pepper, cracked
- 6 tablespoons salt
- 6 tablespoons chili powder
- 1/2 cup smoked paprika
- 1/2 cup brown sugar
- 12-pound uncured beef brisket

Directions:

1. Remove brisket from your packaging and pat it dry with towels, carefully clean the tissues from the lean side
2. Trim the fat cap down to about 1/4 inch thickness, making sure to leave enough space for the flavor and moisture to seep in
3. Transfer the brisket to a large pan
4. Take a bowl and mix all the dry seasoning, coat all sides of your brisket generously with the seasoning
5. Wrap it up and let it rest in your fridge for 4 hours

6. Pre-heat your Grill to 225 degrees F
7. Take the brisket out and let it cool
8. Transfer brisket to the grill and smoke for 9 hours until the internal temperature reaches 200 degrees F
9. Transfer to a slicing board and seal with foil, let it rest for 2 hours
10. Slice and serve, enjoy!

Coffee Rubbed Brisket

Prep Time: 60 minutes/ Cook Time 1 hour 30 minutes/ Serves: 4

Ingredients:

- 4 pounds beef chuck roast
- Olive oil
- Salt and pepper to taste
- Salted butter, melted

The Rub
- 1 tablespoon onion powder
- 2 tablespoons smoked paprika
- 1 tablespoon garlic powder
- 1 teaspoon chili powder
- 1 teaspoon mustard powder
- 1 teaspoon oregano
- 1 teaspoon coriander
- 1 teaspoon white sugar
- 1 teaspoon dried thyme
- 1 tablespoon salt
- 2 tablespoons brown sugar
- 3/4 cup ground coffee

Directions:

1. Prepare the rub by mixing all of the listed ingredients in a small-sized bowl
2. Brush the roast with the mixture all over with oil and season with pepper
3. Cover well with the rub and let it chill for 24 hours
4. Let the meat come for room temperature
5. Pre-heat your Grill to 275 degrees F and

set it for direct cooking
6. Arrange meat on one side of your grill and cook for 1 and 1/2 hours until internal temperature reaches 125 degrees F
7. Bate with butter and tent with foil, let it sit for 30 minutes more
8. Slice and serve, enjoy!

Bourbon Beef Burgers

Prep Time: 60 minutes/ Cook Time 10 minutes/ Serves: 4

Ingredients:

- 1 pound ground beef

The Rub
- 2 tablespoons onion soup mix
- 2 tablespoons Worcestershire sauce
- 2 tablespoons bourbon
- 1 teaspoon hot sauce
- 4 brioche buns, toasted

Directions:

1. Take a large bowl and mix all ingredients under rubbing alongside beef
2. Shape the meat 4 equally sized patties and make an indent
3. Pre-heat your Grill 375 degrees F and set it to direct cooking
4. Place directly on the grill and cook for 5 minutes on each side until medium-rare
5. Serve burgers inside buns and enjoy!

Buttered Up Ribs

Prep Time: 60 minutes/ Cook Time 120 minutes/ Serves: 4

Ingredients:

- 5 pounds boneless rib-eye roast
- Salt and pepper

The Rub
- 1 cup butter
- 1/4 cup fresh thyme chopped

- 4 garlic cloves, peeled and crushed
- 1/4 cup fresh parsley, chopped
- 1/4 cup fresh tarragon, chopped

Directions:

1. Season beef with salt and pepper
2. Prepare a mixture by taking a small bowl and mixing all the rub ingredients, spread mixture all over beef
3. Pre-heat your Grill to 325 degrees F and set it indirect cooking
4. Place beef on the grate and cook for 1 and 1/2 -2 hours until meat shows an internal temperature of 125 degrees F
5. Transfer cooked meat to a serving platter and place a tent set it for 15-20 minutes
6. Slice thickly and enjoy!

Beer Battered Beef Ribs

Prep Time: 60 minutes/ Cook Time 5-6 hours/ Serves: 4

Ingredients:

- 1 rack beef short ribs

The Rub

- Olive oil
- Salt and pepper to taste
- 1 tablespoon garlic powder
- 1 bottle stout beer

Directions:

1. Peel away membrane from the bone side of your ribs
2. Brush rack with olive oil and season with salt, pepper, and garlic
3. Pre-heat your Grill to 265 degrees F
4. Arrange ribs on the grate (the bone side facing down) and grill for a few hours, flip and cook until both sides have a rich gold brown texture
5. Transfer to disposable aluminum foil and pour over stout beer, secure with foil

and transfer back to the grill
6. Cook for a few hours more until internal temperature reaches 200 degrees F
7. Cut the rack into individual bones and enjoy it!

Feisty Grilled Indian Kebab

Prep Time: 60 minutes/ Cook Time 4-8 hours/ Serves: 4

Ingredients:

- 1 pound beef tenderloin, cut into 1 inch cubes
- 2 pounds strip steak, cut into 1-inch cubes
- 1 large onion, cut into 1-inch cubes
- 1 bell pepper, cut into 1-inch cubes
- 1 zucchini, cut into 1-inch cubes
- 10 ounces cherry tomatoes
- 1/4 cup olive oil
- 1/2 cup steak seasoning

Directions:

1. Take a large-sized bowl and add tenderloin, strip steak, onion, zucchini, bell pepper, tomatoes and mix well with olive oil
2. Season with steak seasoning and stir well, let it marinate for 4-8 hours
3. Pre-heat your Grill to 225 degrees F and set it for direct cooking
4. Make kebabs by skewering the meat and veggies alternatively, place in your Grill and smoke for 45 minutes
5. Once the internal temperature reaches 135 degrees F, serve, and enjoy!

Cedar Plank Pork Chops

Prep Time: 20 minutes/ Cook Time 5 hours / Serves: 4

Ingredients:

- 2 cedar planks, soaked up

- Fresh pieces of bay leaves
- Your favorite JAVA rub
- 1 chicken bouillon cube
- 1/2 cup chicken marinade of your choosing
- 3/4 cup of canola oil
- 4 pork chops, double bone-in

Directions:

1. Soak the planks for about 2 hours before your grilling session
2. Take a bowl and add oil, marinade, cube and blend for 45 seconds
3. Transfer pork chops to a pan and pours oil over chops
4. Top them up with leaves
5. Turn chops over, making sure that they are fully coated
6. Let them sit for 3-4 hours
7. Remove from marinade and drain them well
8. Season both sides thoroughly
9. Pre-heat your Grill to 400 degrees F
10. Transfer soaked up planks on Grill and heat them for 30 seconds
11. Flip and add seasoned chops to the plank
12. Cook for about 15-20 minutes until the internal temperature reaches 145 degrees F
13. Serve and enjoy!

Molasses Lamb Chops

Prep Time: 20 minutes/ Cook Time 3 hours / Serves: 4

Ingredients:

- 1/2 cup dry white wine
- 1 cup molasses for honey
- 4 tablespoons molasses
- 4 tablespoon fresh mint, minced
- Salt and pepper to taste

- 2 pounds lamb

Directions:

1. Take a bowl and add molasses, wine, fresh mint, salt and pepper
2. Season cut side of the boned lamb with salt and pepper, spread molasses mixture and roll and tie the lamb
3. Brush outer surface with molasses mixture
4. Pre-heat your Grill to 225 degrees F
5. Lay meat on top rack and smoke until the internal temperature reaches 150 degrees F
6. Remove chops and let it cool for 15 minutes
7. Serve and enjoy!

Herbed Pork Ribs

Prep Time: 20 minutes/ Cook Time 1 hour / Serves: 4

Ingredients:

- 3-4 pounds pork short ribs
- 1/2 cup Dijon mustard
- 6 tablespoons rosemary, dried
- 1/2 cup thyme, dried
- 2 tablespoons oregano, dried
- 2 tablespoons salt
- 1 tablespoon pepper
- 3/4 cup honey
- 10 garlic cloves
- 3 lemons, juiced

Directions:

1. Take a mortar and pestle and add garlic, pepper, herbs, and salt
2. Mash well to form a paste
3. Rub the ribs with the mustard, making sure to cover all sides
4. Let them sit for 45 minutes
5. Take a small-sized bowl and add lemon juice, honey

6. Pre-heat your Grill to 325 degrees F and bring the set it for indirect cooking
7. Transfer ribs to the opposite side of your Grilland cooks them until the internal temperature reaches 180 degrees F
8. Brush with the honey mix
9. Remove ribs once the internal temperature reaches 195 degrees F
10. Brush with more lemon and honey
11. Let them rest for 15 minutes
12. Enjoy!

Mouth-Watering Osso Buco

Prep Time: 20 minutes/ Cook Time 7 hours / Serves: 4

Ingredients:

- 2 large-sized beef shanks
- Kosher salt as needed
- Pepper as needed
- Garlic powder as needed
- Onion powder as needed
- Ground thyme as needed
- 1 tablespoon of vegetable oil
- 1/2 a cup of chopped up onion
- 2 chopped up stalks of celery
- 2 peeled and chopped carrots
- 3 minced garlic cloves
- 1 cup of dry red wine
- 1 cup of beef broth
- 1/3 cup of chopped kalamata olives
- 2 cups of diced tomatoes
- 1 – 6 ounce can of tomato paste
- 1 teaspoon of kosher salt
- 1 teaspoon of course ground black pepper
- 1 bay leaf

Directions:

1. Heat your grill/Grill to a temperature of 275 degrees Fahrenheit
2. Season your beef shanks properly by rubbing them with salt, garlic powder, onion powder and thyme on both sides
3. Place your prepared shanks on your Grill grate
4. Smoke them for 4 hours
5. Take a large-sized a cast iron pot and place it over medium heat on a stove
6. Add celery, onions, carrots, and garlic and Sauté them for until properly softened
7. Add the rest of the ingredients and mix them well
8. Add your prepared shanks into the pot and place the pot over your Grill
9. Smoke for 3 hours more at 275 degrees Fahrenheit
10. Once done, take it out and serve with some polenta or pasta!

Lamb Cutlets Garlic Sauce

Prep Time: 20 minutes/ Cook Time 3 hours / Serves: 4

Ingredients:

- 6 garlic cloves
- 2 tablespoons apple cider vinegar
- 1/2 cup of water
- 1/4 cup extra virgin olive oil
- 1 teaspoon salt
- 1 teaspoon pepper
- 4 pounds lamb cutlets

Directions:

1. Take a bowl and add minced garlic, vinegar, water, olive oil, salt, and pepper
2. Rub the mixture thoroughly over lamb cutlets and transfer them to your fridge, let them chill for4 hours
3. Remove from fridge and let them sit for 45 minutes
4. Take your drip pan and add water, cover with aluminum foil. Pre-heat your Grill to

225 degrees F

5. Use water fill water pan halfway through and place it over drip pan. Add wood chips to the side tray
6. Place meat on the top rack and smoke for 3 hours or until the internal temperature reaches 150 degrees F
7. Remove chops and let them cool for 15 minutes
8. Serve and enjoy!

The Satisfying Pork Butt

Prep Time: 20 minutes/ Cook Time 18 hours / Serves: 4

Ingredients:

- 7 pound of fresh pork butt roast
- 2 tablespoon of ground New Mexico Chile Powder
- 4 tablespoon of packed cup brown sugar

Directions:

1. Soak your pork butt in the brine solution for 4 hours
2. Make sure to cover the butt before placing in your fridge
3. Pre-heat your Grill to 225 degrees F and set it for indirect cooking
4. Take a small bowl and add chili powder, brown sugar alongside any other seasoning that you may fancy
5. Rub butt with your mixture
6. Take the butt and transfer to your Grill, place dripping pan
7. Smoke for 6-10 hours, the internal temperature should reach 100 degrees F

Bourbon Dredged Beef Roast

Prep Time: 20 minutes/ Cook Time 60 minutes per pound / Serves: 4

Ingredients:

- 1/2 a cup of firmly packed light brown sugar
- 1/2 a cup of soy sauce
- 1/2 a cup of olive oil
- 1/2 a cup of bourbon
- 1 lemon juice
- 1 tablespoon of freshly ground black pepper
- 1 whole 3-4 pound of beef roast

Directions:

1. Take a medium bowl and whisk in brown sugar, soy sauce, bourbon, olive oil, lemon juice, and pepper
2. Mix well
3. Transfer the marinade to a large bowl and add meat and marinade
4. Cover with plastic wrap and chill overnight
5. Pre-heat your Grill to 225 degrees Fahrenheit
6. Remove the meat from bowl and discard marinade
7. Transfer roast to Grill rack and smoke for 1 hour per pound (in our case, 3-4 pound should take about 4 hours)
8. Remove the heat once the internal temperature reaches 145 degrees Fahrenheit

The Korean "EYE" BBQ

Prep Time: 20 minutes/ Cook Time 15 minutes per pound / Serves: 4

Ingredients:

- 1/4 cup of soy sauce
- 1/4 cup of chopped scallions
- 2 tablespoon of minced garlic
- 2 tablespoon of gochujang Korean chili paste
- 1 tablespoon of honey
- 2 teaspoon of ground ginger

- 2 teaspoon of onion powder
- 2 boneless 8-12 ounce of rib-eye steaks
- Smoker coleslaw
- 12 flour tortillas

Directions:

1. Pre-heat your Grill to 200 degrees Fahrenheit
2. Take a small bowl and whisk in soy sauce, garlic, scallion, honey, ginger, onion powder, and mix to make the paste
3. Spread the paste on both sides of the steak
4. Transfer the steak to your Grill and smoke for 15 minutes per pound
5. Remove the steak when the internal temperature reaches 115 degrees Fahrenheit
6. Cut the steak into strips and serve with coleslaw wrapped in tortillas
7. Enjoy!

Garlic And Herbed Lamb Rack

Prep Time: 20 minutes/ Cook Time 5-10 minutes / Serves: 16

Ingredients:

- 2 racks lamb

The Rub
- 1/2 bunch fresh rosemary, needles removed
- 1/2 bunch fresh thyme leaves, chopped
- 6 garlic cloves, peeled and minced
- Salt and pepper to taste
- Mustard as needed

Directions:

1. Add the rub ingredients in a bowl
2. Brush a thin layer of mustard over racks and coat with herb mixture
3. Pre-heat your Grill to 355 degrees F and set it for direct cooking

4. Arrange lamb on grill and lock lid, cook for 8 minutes, making sure to turn after every 2 minutes
5. Let the lamb cook for 15 minutes more until the internal temperature reaches 120 degrees F
6. Take lamb racks off the grill and make a foil tent, let it rest for a few minutes
7. Slice and serve
8. Enjoy!

Chapter 2: Poultry Recipes

grilled Chicken Kabobs

Prep time: 45 minutes, Cook time: 12 minutes; Serves: 6

Ingredients

- 1/2 cup olive oil
- 2 tbsp white vinegar
- 1 tbsp lemon juice
- 1-1/2 tbsp salt
- 1/2 tbsp pepper, coarsely ground
- 2 tbsp chives, freshly chopped
- 1-1/2 tbsp thyme, freshly chopped
- 2 tbsp Italian parsley freshly chopped
- 1tbsp garlic, minced

Kabobs

- 1 each orange, red, and yellow pepper
- 1-1/2 lb chicken breast, boneless and skinless
- 12 crimini mushrooms

Preparation Method

1. In a mixing bowl, add all the marinade ingredients and mix well. Toss the chicken and mushrooms in the marinade then refrigerate for 30 minutes.
2. Meanwhile, soak the skewers in hot water. Remove the chicken from the fridge and start assembling the kabobs.
3. Preheat your Smoker to 450°F.
4. Grill the kabobs in the Smoker for 6 minutes, flip them and grill for 6 more minutes.
5. Remove from the grill and let rest. Heat up the naan bread on the grill for 2 minutes.
6. Serve and enjoy.

grilled Chicken

Prep time: 10 minutes, Cook time: 1 hour 10 minutes; Serves: 6

Ingredients

- 5 lb whole chicken
- 1/2 cup oil
- Chicken rub

Preparation Method

1. Preheat your Smoker with the lid open for 5 minutes. Close the lid, increase the temperature to 450°F and preheat for 15 more minutes.
2. Tie the chicken legs together with the baker's twine then rub the chicken with oil and coat with chicken rub.
3. Place the chicken on the grill with the breast side up.
4. Grill the chicken for 70 minutes without opening it or until the internal temperature reaches 165°F.
5. Remove the chicken from the grill and let it rest for 15 minutes before serving.
6. Enjoy.

Smoked Spatchcock Turkey

Prep time: 30 minutes, Cook time: 1 hour 45 minutes; Serves: 6

Ingredients

- 1 whole turkey
- 1/2 cup oil
- 1/4 cup chicken rub
- 1 tbsp onion powder
- 1 tbsp garlic powder
- 1 tbsp rubbed sage

1. Preheat your grill to high.
2. Meanwhile, place the turkey on a platter with the breast side down then cut on either side of the backbone to remove the spine.
3. Flip the turkey and season on both sides then place it on the preheated grill or on a pan if you want to catch the drippings.
4. Grill on high for 30 minutes, reduce the temperature to 325°F, and grill for 45 more minutes or until the internal temperature reaches 165°F
5. Remove from the grill and let rest for 20 minutes before slicing and serving. Enjoy.

Smoked Cornish Hens

Prep time: 10 minutes, Cook time: 1 hour; Serves: 6

Ingredients

- 6 cornish hens
- 3 tbsp avocado oil
- 6 tbsp rub of choice

Preparation Method

1. Fire up the Smoker and preheat it to 275°F.
2. Rub the hens with oil then coat generously with rub. Place the hens on the grill with the chest breast side down.
3. Smoke for 30 minutes. Flip the hens and increase the grill temperature to 400°F. Cook until the internal temperature reaches 165°F.
4. Remove from the grill and let rest for 10 minutes before serving. Enjoy.

Smoked and fried chicken wings

Prep time: 10 minutes, Cook time: 2 hours; Serves: 6

Ingredients

- 3 lb chicken wings
- 1 tbsp goya adobo all-purpose seasoning
- Sauce of your choice

Preparation Method

1. Fire up your grill and set it to smoke.
2. Meanwhile, coat the chicken wings with adobo all-purpose seasoning. Place the chicken on the grill and smoke for 2 hours ensuring you turn halfway through the smoke.
3. Remove the wings from the grill.
4. Preheat oil to 375°F in a frying pan. Drop the wings in batches and let fry for 5 minutes or until the skin is crispy.
5. Remove from oil and let drain before serving with your favorite sauce. Enjoy.

grilled Buffalo Chicken Leg

Prep time: 5 minutes, Cook time: 25 minutes; Serves: 6

Ingredients

- 12 chicken legs
- 1/2 tbsp salt
- 1 tbsp buffalo seasoning
- 1 cup buffalo sauce

Preparation Method

1. Preheat your grill to 325°F.
2. Toss the legs in salt and buffalo seasoning then place them on the preheated grill.
3. Grill for 40 minutes ensuring you turn them twice through the cooking.
4. Brush the legs with buffalo sauce and cook for an additional 10 minutes or until the internal temperature reaches 165°F.
5. Remove the legs from the grill, brush with more sauce, and serve when hot. Enjoy with ranch, celery or blue cheese.

Smoked Chile Lime Chicken

Prep time: 2 minutes, Cook time: 15 minutes;
Serves: 1

- Ingredients
- 1 chicken breast
- 1 tbsp oil
- 1 tbsp chile-lime seasoning

Preparation Method

1. Preheat your Smoker to 400°F.
2. Brush the chicken breast with oil on all sides.
3. Sprinkle with seasoning and salt to taste.
4. Grill for 7 minutes per side or until the internal temperature reaches 165°F.
5. Serve when hot or cold and enjoy.

Smoked Sheet pan Chicken Fajitas

Prep time: 10 minutes, Cook time: 10 minutes;
Serves: 10

Ingredients

- 2 tbsp oil
- 2 tbsp chile margarita seasoning
- 1 tbsp salt
- 1/2 tbsp onion powder
- 1/2 tbsp garlic, granulated
- 2 lb chicken breast, thinly sliced
- 1 red bell pepper, seeded and sliced
- 1 orange bell pepper
- 1 onion, sliced

Preparation Method

1. Preheat the Smoker to 450°F.
2. Meanwhile, mix oil and seasoning then toss the chicken and the peppers.
3. Line a sheet pan with foil then place it in the preheated grill. Let it heat for 10 minutes with the grill's lid closed.
4. Open the grill and place the chicken with the veggies on the pan in a single layer.

5. Cook for 10 minutes or until the chicken is cooked and no longer pink.
6. Remove from grill and serve with tortilla or your favorite fixings.

Buffalo Chicken Flatbread

Prep time: 5 minutes, Cook time: 30 minutes;
Serves: 6

Ingredients

- 6 mini pita bread
- 1-1/2 cups buffalo sauce
- 4 cups chicken breasts, cooked and cubed
- 3 cups mozzarella cheese
- Blue cheese for drizzling

Preparation Method

1. Preheat the grill to 375-400°F.
2. Place the breads on a flat surface and evenly spread sauce over all of them.
3. In a mixing bowl, toss the chicken with the remaining buffalo sauce and place them on the pita breads.
4. Top with cheese then place the breads on the grill but indirectly from the heat. Closs the grill lid.
5. Cook for 7 minutes or until the cheese has melted and the edges are toasty.
6. Remove from grill and drizzle with blue cheese. Serve and enjoy.

grilled Buffalo Chicken

Prep time: 5 minutes, Cook time: 20 minutes;
Serves: 6

Ingredients

- 5 chicken breasts, boneless and skinless
- 2 tbsp homemade bbq rub
- 1 cup homemade Cholula buffalo sauce

Preparation Method

1. Preheat the grill to 400°F.
2. Slice the chicken into long strips and

season with bbq rub.

3. Place the chicken on the grill and paint both sides with buffalo sauce.
4. Cook for 4 minutes with the grill closed. Cook while flipping and painting with buffalo sauce every 5 minutes until the internal temperature reaches 165°F.
5. Remove from the grill and serve when warm. Enjoy.

Beer Can Chicken

Prep time: 10 minutes, Cook time: 1 hour 15 minutes; Serves: 6

Ingredients

- 5 lb chicken
- 1/2 cup dry chicken rub
- 1 can beer

Preparation Method

1. Preheat your grill on smoke for 5 minutes with the lid open. Close the lid and preheat the grill until the temperature reaches 450°F.
2. Pour out half of the beer then shove the can in the chicken and use the legs like a tripod.
3. Place the chicken on the grill and grill until the internal temperature reaches 165°F.
4. Remove from the grill and let rest for 20 minutes before serving. Enjoy.

Smoked Chicken wings with spicy Miso

Prep time: 15 minutes, Cook time: 25 minutes; Serves: 6

Ingredients

- 2 lb chicken wings
- 3/4 cup soy
- 1/2 cup pineapple juice

- 1 tbsp sriracha
- 1/8 cup miso
- 1/8 cup gochujang
- 1/2 cup water
- 1/2 cup oil
- togarashi

Preparation Method

1. In a mixing bowl, mix all ingredients then toss the chicken wings until they are well coated.refrigerate for 12 minutes.
2. Preheat your grill to 375°F.
3. Place the chicken wings on the grill grates and close the lid. Cook until the internal temperature reaches 165°F.
4. Remove the wings from the grill and sprinkle with togarashi.
5. Serve when hot and enjoy.

Barbecue Chicken wings

Prep time: 10 minutes, Cook time: 15 minutes; Serves: 4

Ingredients

- Fresh chicken wings
- Salt to taste
- Pepper to taste
- Garlic powder
- Onion powder
- Cayenne
- Paprika
- Seasoning salt
- Bbq sauce to taste

Preparation Method

1. Preheat the grill to low.
2. In a mixing bowl, mix all the seasoning ingredients then toss the chicken wings until well coated.
3. Place the wings on the grill and cook for 20 minutes or until the wings are fully cooked.
4. Let rest to cool for 5 minutes then toss

with bbq sauce.

5. Serve with orzo and salad. Enjoy.

Bacon-wrapped Chicken Tenders

Prep time: 25 minutes, Cook time: 30 minutes; Serves: 6

Ingredients

- 1 lb chicken tenders
- 10 strips bacon
- 1/2 tbsp Italian seasoning
- 1/2 tbsp black pepper
- 1/2 tbsp salt
- 1 tbsp paprika
- 1 tbsp onion powder
- 1 tbsp garlic powder
- 1/3 cup light brown sugar
- 1 tbsp chili powder

Preparation Method

1. Preheat your Smokerto 350°F.
2. In a mixing bowl, mix Italian seasoning, black pepper, salt, paprika, onion, and garlic until well mixed.
3. Sprinkle the mixture on all sides of the chicken tenders and ensure they are well covered.
4. Wrap each chicken tender with a strip of bacon and tuck the ends.
5. Mix sugar and chili then sprinkle the mixture on the bacon-wrapped chicken.
6. Place them on the smoker and smoker for 30 minutes with the lid closed or until the chicken is cooked.
7. If you desire more crispiness, place the chicken on a baking sheet and broil for a few minutes.
8. Serve and enjoy.

Grilled Chicken

Prep time: 10 minutes, Cook time: 1 hour 10 minutes; Serves 6

Ingredients

- 5 lb. whole chicken
- 1/2 cup oil
- Traeger chicken rub

Preparation Method

1. Preheat the Grill on the smoke setting with the lid open for 5 minutes. Close the lid and let it heat for 15 minutes or until it reaches 450.
2. Use bakers twine to tie the chicken legs together then rub it with oil. Coat the chicken with the rub and place it on the grill.
3. Grill for 70 minutes with the lid closed or until it reaches an internal temperature of 165°F.
4. Remove the chicken from the Grill and let rest for 15 minutes. Cut and serve.

Grilled Chicken Breast

Prep time: 10 minutes, Cook time: 15 minutes; Serves 6

Ingredients

- 3 chicken breasts
- 1 tbsp avocado oil
- 1/4 tbsp garlic powder
- 1/4 tbsp onion powder
- 3/4 tbsp salt
- 1/4 tbsp pepper

Preparation Method

1. Preheat your Grillto 375°F
2. Cut the chicken breast into halves lengthwise then coat with avocado oil.
3. Season with garlic powder, onion powder, salt, and pepper.
4. Place the chicken on the grill and cook for 7 minutes on each side or until the internal temperature reaches 165°F

Smoked Spatchcock Turkey

Prep time: 30 minutes, Cook time: 1 hour 15 minutes; Serves 8

Ingredients

- 1 turkey
- 1/2 cup melted butter
- 1/4 cup Traeger chicken rub
- 1 tbsp onion powder
- 1 tbsp garlic powder
- 1 tbsp rubbed sage

Preparation Method

1. Preheat your Grillto high temperature.
2. Place the turkey on a chopping board with the breast side down and the legs pointing towards you.
3. Cut either side of the turkey backbone, to remove the spine. Flip the turkey and place it on a pan
4. Season both sides with the seasonings and place it on the grill skin side up on the grill.
5. Cook for 30 minutes, reduce temperature, and cook for 45 more minutes or until the internal temperature reaches 165°F.
6. Remove from the Grilland let rest for 15 minutes before slicing and serving.

Smoked Cornish Hens

Prep time: 10 minutes, Cook time: 1 hour; Serves 6

Ingredients

- 6 Cornish hens
- 3 tbsp canola oil
- 6 tbsp rub

Preparation Method

1. Preheat your Grillto 275°F.
2. Meanwhile, rub the hens with canola oil then with your favorite rub.
3. Place the hens on the grill with the breast side down. Smoke for 30 minutes.
4. Flip the hens and increase the Grilltemperature to 400°F. Cook until the internal temperature reaches 165°F.
5. Remove the hens from the grill and let rest for 10 minutes before serving.

Smoked and Fried Chicken wings

Prep time: 10 minutes, Cook time: 2 hours; Serves 4

Ingredients

- 3 lb chicken wings
- 1 tbsp goya adobo seasoning
- Your favorite sauce

Preparation Method

1. Fire up your Grillto smoke setting
2. Generously coat the wings with adobo seasoning then place them on the grill.
3. Smoke them for 2 hours turning them at least once during smoking.
4. Remove the wings from the smoker and heat oil to 375°F.
5. Drop the wings in the hot oil and fry for 5 minutes or until the skin is crispy.
6. Remove the wings from the oil and drain them. Toss in your favorite sauce then serve.

Grilled Buffalo Chicken Legs

Prep time: 30 minutes, Cook time: 1 hour 15 minutes; Serves 8

Ingredients

- 12 chicken legs
- 1/2 tbsp salt
- 1 tbsp buffalo seasoning
- 1 cup Buffalo sauce

1. Preheat your Grillto 325⁰F.
2. Toss the chicken legs in salt and seasoning then place them on the preheated grill.
3. Grill for 40 minutes turning twice through the cooking.
4. Increase the heat and cook for 10 more minutes. Brush the chicken legs and brush with buffalo sauce. Cook for an additional 10 minutes or until the internal temperature reaches 165⁰F.
5. Remove from the Grilland brush with more buffalo sauce.
6. Serve with blue cheese, celery, and hot ranch.

Grilled Chile Lime Chicken

Prep time: 2 minutes, Cook time: 15 minutes; Serves 1

Ingredients

- 1 chicken breast
- 1 tbsp oil
- 1 tbsp spiceology Chile Lime Seasoning

Preparation Method

1. Preheat your Grill to 400⁰F.
2. Brush the chicken breast with oil then sprinkle the chile-lime seasoning and salt.
3. Place the chicken breast on the grill and cook for 7 minutes on each side or until the internal temperature reaches 165⁰F.
4. Serve when hot and enjoy.

Grilled Buffalo Chicken

Prep time: 5 minutes, Cook time: 20 minutes; Serves 6

Ingredients

- 5 chicken breasts, boneless and skinless

- 2 tbsp homemade BBQ rub
- 1 cup homemade Cholula Buffalo sauce

Preparation Method

1. Preheat the Grill to 400⁰F.
2. Slice the chicken breast lengthwise into strips. Season the slices with BBQ rub.
3. Place the chicken slices on the grill and paint both sides with buffalo sauce.
4. Cook for 4 minutes with the lid closed. Flip the breasts, paint again with sauce and cook until the internal temperature reaches 165⁰F.
5. Remove the chicken from the Grill and serve when warm.

Grilled Sheet Pan Chicken Fajitas

Prep time: 10 minutes, Cook time: 10 minutes; Serves 10

Ingredients

- 2 lb chicken breast
- 1 onion, sliced
- 1 red bell pepper, seeded and sliced
- 1 orange-red bell pepper, seeded and sliced
- 1 tbsp salt
- 1/2 tbsp onion powder
- 1/2 tbsp granulated garlic
- 2 tbsp Spiceologist Chile Margarita Seasoning
- 2 tbsp oil

Preparation Method

1. Preheat the Grill to 450⁰F and line a baking sheet with parchment paper.
2. In a mixing bowl, combine seasonings and oil then toss with the peppers and chicken.
3. Place the baking sheet in the Grill and let heat for 10 minutes with the lid closed.
4. Open the lid and place the veggies and the chicken in a single layer. Close the

lid and cook for 10 minutes or until the chicken is no longer pink.

5. Serve with warm tortillas and top with your favorite toppings.

Grilled Asian Miso Chicken wings

Prep time: 15 minutes, Cook time: 25 minutes; Serves 6

Ingredients

- 2 lb chicken wings
- 3/4 cup soy
- 1/2 cup pineapple juice
- 1 tbsp sriracha
- 1/8 cup miso
- 1/8 cup gochujang
- 1/2 cup water
- 1/2 cup oil
- Togarashi

Preparation Method

1. Preheat the Grill to 375^0F
2. Combine all the ingredients except togarashi in a zip lock bag. Toss until the chicken wings are well coated. Refrigerate for 12 hours
3. Pace the wings on the grill grates and close the lid. Cook for 25 minutes or until the internal temperature reaches 165^0F
4. Remove the wings from the Grill and sprinkle Togarashi.
5. Serve when hot and enjoy.

Chicken And Guacamole

Prep Time: 20 minutes/ Cook Time 1 hour / Serves: 4

Ingredients:

- 2 chicken breasts
- 2 avocado, ripe
- 1 tomato, diced
- 1 lime
- 1 teaspoon salt
- 1 teaspoon garlic powder
- 1 teaspoon Cajun
- 4 multigrain bread, slices

Directions:

1. Pre-heat your Grill to 225 degrees F
2. Apply Cajun seasoning generously to your chicken breasts
3. Add chicken inside your Grill and smoke for 1 and ½ hours until internal temperature reaches 165 degrees F
4. Once done, remove chicken and keep it on the side, let it rest for 10 minutes. Slice up
5. Cut into avocado into halves and remove seeds, scoop out the flesh into a medium sized bowl
6. Squeeze half lemon into the avocado and mix we, spoon to remove all lumps and bring to a smooth mix
7. Add in chopped tomatoes and onions and stir
8. Pour rest of the lime juice over avocado mix and season with salt and pepper
9. Take a slice of multigrain and place chicken and salad mix on top, top with another slice, and enjoy!

Greek Herbed Chicken

Prep Time: 20 minutes/ Cook Time 20-30 minutes / Serves: 4

Ingredients:

- 3 and 1/2 pounds roasting chicken

The Rub

- 1/4 cup of water
- 2 chicken stock cubes
- 1/2 cup fresh lemon juice
- 1 tablespoon lemon pepper seasoning
- 1/2 cup canola oil seasoning

- 1 tablespoon dried oregano
- Zest of 1 lemon
- 1/4 cup fresh parsley, chopped
- Chicken stock

Directions:

1. Prepare the seasoning by mixing all the ingredients in a bowl and blending it using an immersion blender
2. Place chicken in a stainless steel bowl and pour the marinade, let it chill for 4 hours, making a sure turn it a few times
3. Take chicken out and drip excess
4. Pre-heat your Grill to 350 degrees F
5. Arrange chicken on vertical roasted and fill with beer/chicken stock
6. Arrange vertical roaster inside a roasting tin to catch any dripping
7. Arrange on the cooking grid
8. Cook until the internal temperature reaches 165 degrees F
9. Serve and enjoy!

Rosemary Chicken Kebobs

Prep Time: 20 minutes/ Cook Time 10 minutes / Serves: 4

Ingredients:

- 5 boneless, skinless chicken breasts, cubed

The Rub

- 1/2 cup ranch dressing
- 1/2 cup olive oil
- 1 tablespoon fresh rosemary, minced
- 3 tablespoons Worcestershire sauce
- 1 teaspoon lemon juice
- 2 teaspoons salt
- 1/4 teaspoon pepper
- 1 teaspoon white vinegar
- 1 tablespoon sugar

Directions:

1. Prepare marinade by adding ranch

dressing, olive oil, rosemary, sauce, lemon juice, salt, vinegar, sugar in a bowl and mix well
2. Let it stand for a while
3. Add chicken and toss well, let it chill for 30 minutes
4. Thread cubes onto skewers and arrange on a lightly oiled grid
5. Pre-heat your Grill to 400 degrees F and set it for direct cooking
6. Grill for 10 minutes until cook well
7. Enjoy!

Turkey Parmigiana

Prep Time: 20 minutes/ Cook Time 30 minutes / Serves: 4

Ingredients:

- 1 pound turkey breast fillets, boneless

The Rub

- 2 egg whites
- 1 tablespoon water
- 2 tablespoons Italian seasoned breadcrumbs
- 2 tablespoons parmesan cheese
- 1 cup marinara sauce
- 1 cup mozzarella sauce, shredded

Directions:

1. Whisk in egg whites and water in a shallow dish, take another dish and add breadcrumbs and parmesan
2. Dip each turkey fillet first in egg whites and then in bread crumbs
3. Arrange the meat in pan and place on cooking
4. Pre-heat your Grill to 400 degrees F and set it for in-direct cooking
5. Cook for 30 minutes, pour marinara sauce over breaded turkey and sprinkle over mozzarella
6. Cook for 5 minutes more until cheese

melts. Enjoy!

Parmesan Chicken Legs

Prep Time: 20 minutes/ Cook Time 20-40 minutes / Serves: 4

Ingredients:

- 1/2 cup parmesan cheese
- 3 tablespoons garlic powder
- 1/2 cup butter, melted
- 1/2 cup chicken wing rub, your choice
- 6 chicken legs

Directions:

1. Pre-heat your Grill to 375 degrees F
2. Season chicken legs with wing rub, mix in butter and garlic well
3. Add chicken to Grill, keep cooking until the internal temperature is 165 degrees F, making sure to flip it after every 5 minutes
4. Remove and transfer to Iron Skillet
5. Sprinkle parmesan cheese and cook for 10-15 minutes more until the cheese melts completely
6. Enjoy!

Praiseworthy Buddha's Chicken Wing

Prep Time: 20 minutes/ Cook Time 20-30 minutes / Serves: 4

Ingredients:

- 1 pound chicken wings
- 1 tablespoon vegetable oil
- 1 cup onion sriracha BBQ sauce
- 2 tablespoons smoke and sweet seasoning

Directions:

1. Pre-heat your Grill to 350 degrees F
2. Drizzle wings with oil and add seasoning, toss well

3. Add seasoned wings to Grill and close dome, cook for about 30 minutes, flip and cook for 20 minutes more
4. Remove Grill
5. Increase the temperature to 400 degrees F
6. Coat wings with Onion Sriracha Sauce, transfer them back to Grill and cook for 5 minutes more until caramelized
7. Remove Wings and let them rest
8. Enjoy!

Turkey Breast

Prep Time: 20 minutes/ Cook Time 3-4 hours / Serves: 4

Ingredients:

- 4 tablespoons of unsalted butter
- 8 teaspoon of Dijon mustard
- 2 tablespoon of chopped fresh thyme leaves
- 1 teaspoon of freshly ground black pepper
- 1/2 a teaspoon of kosher salt
- 1 bone-in turkey breast

Directions:

1. Take a small-sized bowl and stir in butter, thyme, mustard, 1/4 teaspoon of pepper, salt
2. Rub the turkey breast with the butter mix
3. Cover and allow it to refrigerate overnight
4. Pre-heat your Grill to 250 degrees Fahrenheit
5. Sprinkle breast with 3/4 teaspoon of pepper and transfer to Grill rack
6. Cover and smoke for 3 and a 1/2 to 4 hours, making sure to keep adding more chips after every 60 minutes
7. Once the internal temperature reaches

Chapter 3: Seafood Recipes

Smoked salmon

Prep time: 10 minutes, Cook time: 4 hours;
Serves: 8

Ingredients

Brine
- 4 cups water
- 1 cup brown sugar
- 1/3 cup kosher salt

Salmon
- Salmon fillet, skin in
- Maple syrup

Preparation Method

1. Combine all the brine ingredients until the sugar has fully dissolved.
2. Add the brine to a ziplock bag with the salmon and refrigerate for 12 hours.
3. Remove the salmon from the brine, wash it and rinse with water. Pat dry with paper towel then let sit at room temperature for 2 hours.
4. Startup your Smoker to smoke and place the salmon on a baking rack sprayed with cooking spray.
5. After cooking for an hour, baste the salmon with maple syrup. Do not let the smoker get above 180°F for accurate results.
6. Smoke for 3-4 hours or until the salmon flakes easily.

Smoked Teriyaki Smoked Shrimp

Prep time: 10 minutes, Cook time: 10 minutes;
Serves: 6

Ingredients
- 1 lb tail-on shrimp, uncooked
- 1/2 tbsp onion powder
- 1/2 tbsp salt
- 1/2 tbsp Garlic powder
- 4 tbsp Teriyaki sauce
- 4 tbsp sriracha mayo
- 2 tbsp green onion, minced

Preparation Method

1. Peel the shrimps leaving the tails then wash them removing any vein left over. Drain and pat with a paper towel to drain.
2. Preheat the Smoker to 450°F
3. Season the shrimp with onion, salt, and garlic then place it on the grill to cook for 5 minutes on each side.
4. Remove the shrimp from the grill and toss it with teriyaki sauce. Serve garnished with mayo and onions. Enjoy.

grilled Scallops

Prep time: 5 minutes, Cook time: 15 minutes;
Serves: 4

Ingredients
- 2 lb sea scallops, dried with a paper towel
- 1/2 tbsp garlic salt
- 2 tbsp kosher salt
- 4 tbsp salted butter
- Squeeze lemon juice

Preparation Method

1. Preheat the grill to 400°F with the cast pan inside.
2. Sprinkle with both salts, pepper on both sides of the scallops.

3. Place the butter on the cast iron then add the scallops. Close the lid and cook for 8 minutes.
4. Flip the scallops and close the lid once more. Cook for 8 more minutes.
5. Remove the scallops from the grill and give a lemon squeeze. Serve immediately and enjoy.

Grilled Shrimp Scampi

Prep time: 5 minutes, Cook time: 10 minutes; Serves: 4

Ingredients

- 1 lb raw shrimp, tail on
- 1/2 cup salted butter, melted
- 1/4 cup white wine, dry
- 1/2 tbsp fresh garlic, chopped
- 1 tbsp lemon juice
- 1/2 tbsp garlic powder
- 1/2 tbsp salt

Preparation Method

1. Preheat your grill to 400°F with a cast iron inside.
2. In a mixing bowl, mix butter, wine, garlic, and juice then pour in the cast iron. Let the mixture mix for 4 minutes.
3. Sprinkle garlic and salt on the shrimp then place it on the cast iron. Grill for 10 minutes with the lid closed.
4. Remove the shrimp from the grill and serve when hot. Enjoy.

Smoked Buffalo Shrimp

Prep time: 10 minutes, Cook time: 5 minutes; Serves: 6

Ingredients

- 1 lb raw shrimps peeled and deveined
- 1/2 tbsp salt
- 1/4 tbsp garlic salt
- 1/4 tbsp garlic powder

- 1/4 tbsp onion powder
- 1/2 cup buffalo sauce

Preparation Method

1. Preheat the grill to 450°F.
2. Coat the shrimp with both salts, garlic and onion powders.
3. Place the shrimp in a grill and cook for 3 minutes on each side.
4. Remove from the grill and toss in buffalo sauce. Serve with cheese, celery and napkins. Enjoy.

grilled Salmon Sandwich

Prep time: 10 minutes, Cook time: 15 minutes; Serves: 4

Ingredients

Salmon Sandwiches
- 4 salmon fillets
- 1 tbsp olive oil
- Fin and feather rub
- 1 tbsp salt
- 4 toasted bun
- Butter lettuce

Dill Aioli
- 1/2 cup mayonnaise
- 1/2 tbsp lemon zest
- 2 tbsp lemon juice
- 1/4 tbsp salt
- 1/2 tbsp fresh dill, minced

Preparation Method

1. Mix all the dill aioli ingredients and place them in the fridge.
2. Preheat the grill to 450°F.
3. Brush the salmon fillets with oil, rub, and salt. Place the fillets on the grill and cook until the internal temperature reaches 135°F.
4. Remove the fillets from the grill and let rest for 5 minutes.
5. Spread the aioli on the buns then top

with salmon, lettuce, and the top bun.
6. Serve when hot.

Grilled Teriyaki salmon

Prep time: 10 minutes, Cook time: 30 minutes; Serves: 4

Ingredients

- 1 salmon fillet
- 1/8 cup olive oil
- 1/2 tbsp salt
- 1/4 tbsp pepper
- 1/4 tbsp garlic salt
- 1/4 cup butter, sliced
- 1/4 teriyaki sauce
- 1 tbsp sesame seeds

Preparation Method

1. Preheat the grill to 400°F.
2. Place the salmon fillet on a non-stick foil sheet. Drizzle the salmon with oil, seasonings, and butter on top.
3. Pace the foil tray on the grill and close the lid. Cook for 8 minutes then open the lid.
4. Brush the salmon with teriyaki sauce and repeat after every 5 minutes until all sauce is finished. The internal temperature should be 145°F.
5. Remove the salmon from the grill and sprinkle with sesame seeds.
6. Serve and enjoy with your favorite side dish.

Smoked Togarashi Grilled Salmon

Prep time: 5 minutes, Cook time: 20 minutes; Serves: 6

Ingredients

- 1 salmon fillet
- 1/4 cup olive oil
- 1/2 tbsp kosher salt
- 1 tbsp Togarashi seasoning

Preparation Method

1. Preheat the grill to 400°F.
2. Place the salmon fillet on a non-stick foil sheet with the skin side up.
3. Rub the olive oil on the salmon and sprinkle with salt and togarashi seasoning.
4. Place the salmon on the preheated grill and close the lid. Cook for 20 minutes or until the internal temperature reaches 145°F.
5. Remove from the grill and serve when hot. Enjoy.

Grilled Lingcod

Prep time: 10 minutes, Cook time: 15 minutes; Serves: 6

Ingredients

- 2 lb lingcod fillets
- 1/2 tbsp salt
- 1/2 tbsp white pepper
- 1/4 tbsp cayenne
- Lemon wedges

Preparation Method

1. Preheat the grill to 375°F.
2. Place the lingcod on a parchment paper and season it with salt, white pepper, cayenne pepper then top with the lemon.
3. Place the fish on the grill and cook for 15 minutes or until the internal temperature reaches 145°F.
4. Serve and enjoy.

Smoked Rockfish

Prep time: 10 minutes, Cook time: 20 minutes; Serves: 6

Ingredients

- 6 rockfish fillets

- 1 lemon, sliced
- 3/4 tbsp Himalayan salt
- 2 tbsp fresh dill, chopped
- 1/2 tbsp garlic powder
- 1/2 tbsp onion powder
- 6 tbsp butter

Preparation Method

1. Preheat your grill to 375°F.
2. Place the rockfish in a baking dish and season with salt, dill, garlic, and onion.
3. Place butter on top of the fish then close the lid. Cook for 20 minutes or until the fish is no longer translucent.
4. Remove from grill and let sit for 5 minutes before serving. enjoy.

Smoked Salt and Pepper Spot Prawn Skewers

Prep time: 10 minutes, Cook time: 10 minutes; Serves: 6

Ingredients

- 2 lb spot prawns, clean
- 2 tbsp oil
- Salt and pepper to taste

Preparation Method

1. Preheat your grill to 400°F.
2. Meanwhile, soak the skewers then skewer with the prawns.
3. Brush with oil then season with salt and pepper to taste.
4. Place the skewers in the grill, close the lid, and cook for 5 minutes on each side.
5. Remove from the grill and serve. Enjoy.

Bacon-wrapped Shrimp

Prep time: 20 minutes, Cook time: 10 minutes; Serves: 12

Ingredients

- 1 lb raw shrimp

- 1/2 tbsp salt
- 1/4 tbsp garlic powder
- 1 lb bacon, halved

Preparation Method

1. Preheat the grill to 350°F.
2. Remove the tail shells on the shrimp placing them on a paper towel.
3. Season the shrimps with salt and garlic then wrap with bacon and secure with a toothpick.
4. Place the shrimps on a baking rack that is coated with cooking spray.
5. Cook for 10 minutes on each side or until you achieve your desired crispiness.
6. Remove from the grill and serve when hot. Enjoy.

Bacon-wrapped Scallops

Prep time: 15 minutes, Cook time: 20 minutes; Serves: 8

Ingredients

- 1 lb sea scallops
- 1/2 lb bacon
- Salt to taste

Preparation Method

1. Preheat your grill to 375°F.
2. Pat dry the scallops with paper towel then wrap with the bacon and secure with a toothpick.
3. Lay the scallops on the grill with the bacon side down. Close the lid and cook for 7 minutes on each side.
4. The bacon should be crispy and scallops tender. Remove from the grill and serve. Enjoy.

grilled Lobster Tail

Prep time: 10 minutes, Cook time: 15 minutes; Serves: 2

Ingredients

- 10 oz lobster tail
- 1/4 tbsp old bay seasoning
- 1/4 tbsp Himalayan sea salt
- 2 tbsp butter, melted
- 1 tbsp fresh parsley, chopped

Preparation Method

1. Preheat the Smoker to 450°F.
2. Slice the tails down the middle using a knife.
3. Season with seasoning and salt then place the tails on the grill grate.
4. Grill for 15 minutes or until the internal temperature reaches 140°F..
5. Remove the tails and drizzle with butter and garnish with parsley.
6. Serve and enjoy.

Smoked Garlic Dill Smoked Salmon

Prep time: 15minutes, Cook time: 4 hours; Serves: 12

Ingredients

- 2 salmon fillets

Brine
- 4 cups water
- 1 cup brown sugar
- 1/3 cup kosher salt

Seasoning
- 3 tbsp minced garlic
- 1 tbsp fresh dill, chopped

Preparation Method

1. In a zip lock bag, combine the brine ingredients until all sugar has dissolved. Place the salmon in the bag and refrigerate overnight.
2. Remove the salmon from the brine, rinse with water and pat dry with a paper towel. Let it rest for 2-4 hours at room temperature.
3. Season the salmon with garlic and dill generously.
4. Fire up the grill to smoke and place the salmon on a cooling rack that is coated with cooking spray.
5. Place the rack in the smoker and close the lid.
6. Smoke the salmon for 4 hours until the smoke is between 130-180°F.
7. Remove the salmon from the grill and serve with crackers. Enjoy

Grilled Salmon with Togarashi

Prep time: 5 minutes, Cook time: 20 minutes; Serves 3

Ingredients

- 1 salmon fillet
- 1/4 cup olive oil
- 1/2 tbsp kosher salt
- 1 tbsp Togarashi seasoning

Preparation Method

1. Preheat your Grill to 400°F.
2. Place the salmon on a sheet lined with non-stick foil with the skin side down.
3. Rub the oil into the meat then sprinkle salt and Togarashi.
4. Place the salmon on the grill and cook for 20 minutes or until the internal temperature reaches 145°F with the lid closed.
5. Remove from the Grill and serve when hot.

Grilled Rockfish

Prep time: 10 minutes, Cook time: 20 minutes; Serves 6

Ingredients

- 6 rockfish fillets

- 1 lemon, sliced
- 3/4 tbsp salt
- 2 tbsp fresh dill, chopped
- 1/2 tbsp garlic powder
- 1/2 tbsp onion powder
- 6 tbsp butter

1. Preheat your Grill to 400^{0}F.
2. Season the fish with salt, dill, garlic and onion powder on both sides then place it in a baking dish.
3. Place a pat of butter and a lemon slice on each fillet. Place the baking dish in the Grill and close the lid.
4. Cook for 20 minutes or until the fish is no longer translucent and is flaky.
5. Remove from Grill and let rest for 5 minutes before serving.

Grilled Lingcod

Prep time: 10 minutes, Cook time: 15 minutes; Serves 6

Ingredients

- 2 lb lingcod fillets
- 1/2 tbsp salt
- 1/2 tbsp white pepper
- 1/4 tbsp cayenne pepper
- Lemon wedges

Preparation Method

1. Preheat your Grill to 375^{0}F.
2. Place the lingcod on a parchment paper or on a grill mat
3. Season the fish with salt, pepper, and top with lemon wedges.
4. Cook the fish for 15 minutes or until the internal temperature reaches 145^{0}F.

Crab Stuffed Lingcod

Prep time: 20 minutes, Cook time: 30 minutes; Serves 6

Ingredients

Lemon cream sauce
- 4 garlic cloves
- 1 shallot
- 1 leek
- 2 tbsp olive oil
- 1 tbsp salt
- 1/4 tbsp black pepper
- 3 tbsp butter
- 1/4 cup white wine
- 1 cup whipping cream
- 2 tbsp lemon juice
- 1 tbsp lemon zest

Crab mix
- 1 lb crab meat
- 1/3 cup mayo
- 1/3 cup sour cream
- 1/3 cup lemon cream sauce
- 1/4 green onion, chopped
- 1/4 tbsp black pepper
- 1/2 tbsp old bay seasoning

Fish
- 2 lb lingcod
- 1 tbsp olive oil
- 1 tbsp salt
- 1 tbsp paprika
- 1 tbsp green onion, chopped
- 1 tbsp Italian parsley

Preparation Method

Lemon cream sauce
1. Chop garlic, shallot, and leeks then add to a saucepan with oil, salt, pepper, and butter.
2. Saute over medium heat until the shallot is translucent.
3. Deglaze with white wine then add whipping cream. Bring the sauce to boil, reduce heat and simmer for 3 minutes.
4. Remove from heat and add lemon juice and lemon zest. Transfer the sauce to a blender and blend until smooth.

- 4 halibuts
- Pecan Rub
- 4 tablespoons clover honey

The Rub
- 1/2 cup of salt
- 1 cup of sugar
- 4 tablespoons cumin
- 1 tablespoon white pepper
- 2 bay leaves crushed
- gallon water

Directions:

1. Prepare to bring by mixing in salt, sugar, cumin, white pepper, bay leaves, water and mix well
2. Pour bring over halibut fillets and keep it on the side for 2 hours
3. Remove halibut and transfer to a kitchen towel, pat dry
4. Season both sides with pecan dry rub, skin side facing down
5. Pre-heat your Grill to 275 degrees F
6. Transfer to Grill skin side facing down, arrange fish fillets directly on cooking grate and smoke until internal temperature reaches 135 degrees F
7. Drizzle fish with warm honey just 10 minutes before completion of cooking
8. Serve and enjoy!

Lemon And Rosemary Grouper

Prep Time: 10 minutes/ Cook Time 20-30 minutes / Serves: 4

Ingredients:

- 3 grouper fillets

The Rub
- 1 tablespoon freshly squeezed lemon juice
- 1/2 teaspoon dried rosemary, crushed
- 1 and 1/2 teaspoons olive oil
- 1/4 teaspoon salt

- Dash of black pepper

Saute
- 1/4 cup tomato, seed and diced
- 1 teaspoon dried basil
- 1 tablespoon green onion, chopped
- 1 and 1/2 teaspoon red wine vinegar

Directions:

1. Take a zip bag and add fresh lemon juice, rosemary, olive oil, salt, and pepper
2. Add fish fillets to bag and seal bag
3. Transfer to fridge and let it chill for 60 minutes
4. Drain and discard marinade
5. Pre-heat your Grill to 350 degrees F and set it for DIRECT cooking
6. Transfer fish to grid and grill both sides until fish fillets flake easily using a fork
7. Take a pan and add sauce ingredients and mix well
8. Place over medium heat and heat it up
9. Serve fish fillets with sauce and enjoy!

Planked Sweet Chili Salmon

Prep Time: 10 minutes/ Cook Time 20-30 minutes / Serves: 4

Ingredients:

- Thai sweet chili sauce of your desire
- Sweet and smoky seasoning as you need
- 2 salmon fillets cut up nicely to fit on a plank

Directions:

1. Pre-heat your Grill to 350 degrees F
2. Place planks in pan and cover with water, let them soak for 2 hours
3. Season the fillets with seasoning, pour Thai sauce to a pot sauce and gently warm
4. Place plank on your Grill 's cooking grid, lock dome and let them heat for about 2

minutes

5. Use tongs to flip the planks and place salmon on plank
6. Coat with sauce and lock dome, let them cook for 20-25 minutes
7. Serve and enjoy!

Crab Cakes With BBQ Ranch Sauce

Prep Time: 10 minutes/ Cook Time 60 minutes / Serves: 4

Ingredients:

- 1 pound lump crabmeat
- 1/2 cup BBQ sauce of your choice
- 1/2 cup ranch dressing

The Rub
- 2 large eggs, beaten
- 2 jalapenos, seeded and minced
- 1/2 cup panko breadcrumbs
- 1/2 cup mayonnaise
- 1 tablespoon fresh parsley, chopped
- 2 teaspoons hot seasoning

Directions:

1. Take a bowl and add eggs, jalapenos, breadcrumbs, mayonnaise, parsley, and hot seasoning to a bowl, mix well
2. Add crab meat to the mixture using clean hands gently combine
3. Form mixture into 4 evenly sized balls using palm and flatten them into patties
4. Pre-heat your Grill to 375 degrees F
5. Transfer to Grill and smoke for 18-20 minutes
6. Take a bowl and mix in BBQ sauce, ranch dressing and serve the sauce. Enjoy!

Honey And Plank Salmon

Prep Time: 10 minutes/ Cook Time 25-30 minutes / Serves: 4

Ingredients:

- 2 cedar grilling planks
- 4 salmon fillets, skin on
- 2 tablespoons extra virgin olive oil
- 1 teaspoon fresh thyme, minced
- tablespoon balsamic vinegar
- teaspoons orange zest, grated
- 1/4 cup honey
- 1/2 cup Dijon mustard
- Salt and pepper to taste

Directions:

1. Place planks in a pan and cover them with water, let them soak for an hour
2. Pre-heat your Grill to 400 degrees F and set it for direct cooking
3. Take a bowl and whisk in mustard, honey, orange zest, 1 teaspoon thyme, vinegar
4. Transfer planks on grids and lock lid, let them heat for 3 minutes
5. Open the lid and turn planks over, brush with oil and add salmon fillets
6. Season with salt and pepper, the brush will with your glaze
7. Cook for 12-15 minutes
8. Enjoy with a garnish with thyme

Homely Seared Tuna

Prep Time: 10 minutes +15 hours/ Cook Time 1 and 1/2 hours / Serves: 4

Ingredients:

- 2 tablespoons sesame seeds, toasted
- 1 teaspoon sriracha
- 1/4 cup honey
- 1/4 cup pineapple juice
- 1 teaspoon corn starch
- 1/4 cup of soy sauce
- 2 ahi tuna steaks

Directions:

1. Pre-heat your Grill to 500 degrees F
2. Take a bowl and mix in cornstarch and

soy sauce, and mix until smooth

3. Add pineapple juice, sriracha, and honey
4. Place pot on your stove over medium heat, bring the mix to a boil
5. Lower down the heat to low and simmer for 3-4 minutes, until it is thick
6. Remove heat
7. Add iron skillet to Grill and add oil, sear tuna steaks, making sure to brush with the mixture
8. Garnish and enjoy!
9. Once done, let it rest for 5 minutes and serve!

Smoked Teriyaki

Prep Time: 10 minutes +15 hours/ Cook Time 2 hours/ Serves: 4

Ingredients:

- 1 ounce of fresh tuna steaks
- 2 cups of teriyaki marinade
- Alder wood chips soaked in water

Directions:

1. Slice the tuna into uniform thick slices of 2 inch each
2. Transfer the tuna slices to a gallon re-sealable bag alongside Teriyaki marinade and transfer them to a shallow baking dish
3. Allow them to refrigerate for 3 hours
4. After 3 hours, remove the tuna from the marinade and pat it dry using a kitchen towel
5. Let the tuna dry in your fridge for 2-4 hours
6. Pre-heat your Grill to 180 degrees Fahrenheit and add chips
7. Transfer to Tuna to a Teflon coated fiberglass and transfer to your Smoker middle rack
8. Smoker for 60 minutes, increase the

temperature to 250 degrees Fahrenheit and Grill for 60 minutes more until the internal temperature reaches 145 degrees Fahrenheit

9. Remove the tuna from Grill and rest for 10 minutes. Enjoy!

Peppercorn Tuna Steaks

Prep Time: 10 minutes / Cook Time 1 hour/ Serves: 4

Ingredients:

- 1 ounce of fresh tuna steaks
- 2 cups of teriyaki marinade
- Alder wood chips soaked in water

Directions:

1. Take a large-sized container and dissolve salt in warm water (enough water to cover fish)
2. Transfer tuna to the brine and cover, refrigerate for 8 hours
3. Pre-heat your Grill to 250 degrees Fahrenheit with your preferred wood
4. Remove tuna from bring and pat it dry
5. Transfer to grill pan and spread Dijon mustard all over
6. Season with pepper and sprinkle peppercorn on top
7. Transfer tuna to Grill and Grill for 1 hour

Pacific Oyster

Prep Time: 10 minutes / Cook Time 2 hours/ Serves: 4

Ingredients:

- 40 to 50 oysters in shells
- 1 cup of white wine
- 1 cup of water
- 1/4 cup of high-quality olive oil

Directions:

1. Wash the oysters under cold water

2. Take a bowl and add white wine, water and bring to a boil
3. Add oysters in a single layer and steam for 3 minutes until the oysters are open
4. Transfer the opened oysters to a bowl and add more fresh ones to the steaming pot. Repeat until all oysters are done
5. Strain the cooking liquid through a paper towel into a bowl and keep the liquid on the side
6. Take a small bowl and sharp knife and remove the oysters from the shells, transfer the removed oysters to the bowl
7. Dip the removed oysters to the cooking liquid and keep them there for 20 minutes
8. Pre-heat your Grill to 145 degrees Fahrenheit
9. Transfer oysters to the middle rack (If possible, keep them on top a grate to ensure that the oysters don't fall off)
10. Smoke for 90 to 120 minutes, making sure to not overcook them
11. Drizzle a bit of olive oil over the oysters and enjoy!

Smoked Sablefish

Prep Time: 15 minutes / Cook Time 3 hours/ Serves: 8

Ingredients:

- 2-3 pounds of sablefish fillets
- 1 cup of kosher salts
- 1/4 cup of sugar
- 2 tablespoon of garlic powder
- Honey for glazing
- Sweet paprika for dusting

Directions:

1. Take a bowl and mix salt, garlic powder, and sugar
2. Pour on a healthy layer of your mix into a lidded plastic tub, enough large to hold the fish
3. Cut up the fillet into pieces
4. Gently massage the salt mix into your fish meat and place them with the skin side down on to the salt mix in the plastic tub
5. Cover up the container and keep it in your fridge for as many hours as the fish weighs
6. Remove the sablefish from the tub and place it under cold water for a while
7. Pat it dries using a kitchen towel and places it back to the fridge, keep it uncovered overnight
8. Pre-heat your Grill to a temperature of 160 degrees Fahrenheit and smoke you fish for 2-3 hours
9. After the first hour of smoking, make sure to baste the fish with honey and keep repeating this after every hour
10. One done, move the fish to a cooling rack and baste it with honey one last time
11. Let it cool for about an hour
12. Use tweezers to pull out the bone pins
13. Dust the top with some paprika and wait for 30 minutes to let the paprika sink in
14. Put the fish in your fridge
15. Serve hot or chilled!

Juicy Salmon Nuggets

Prep Time: 15 minutes / Cook Time 2 hours/ Serves: 8

Ingredients:

- 3 cups of packed brown sugar
- 1 cup of salt
- 1 tablespoon of dry minced onion
- 2 teaspoon of chipotle seasoning
- 2 teaspoon of fresh ground black pepper
- 1 minced garlic cloves
- 1-2 pound of salmon fillets, cut up into

bite-sized portions

Directions:

1. Take a large-sized bowl and stir in brown sugar, salt, chipotle seasoning, onion, garlic and pepper
2. Transfer salmon to a large shallow marinating dish
3. Pour dry marinade over fish and cover, refrigerate overnight
4. Pre-heat your Grill to 180 degrees Fahrenheit
5. Rinse the salmon chunks thoroughly and remove salt
6. Transfer them to grill rack and smoke for 1-2 hours
7. Remove the heat and enjoy it!

Garlic And Citrus Scallops

Prep Time: 15 minutes / Cook Time 30-40 minutes/ Serves: 8

Ingredients:

- 2-3 pounds of fresh scallops
- 1 tablespoon of freshly squeezed lemon juice
- 1 tablespoon of freshly squeezed orange juice
- 1 tablespoon of ground black pepper
- 2 teaspoon of salt
- 1 minced garlic clove
- Zest of 1 orange

Directions:

1. Pre-heat your Grill to 200 degrees Fahrenheit using your desired wood
2. Take a large bowl and stir in scallops with orange juice and lemon
3. Season with salt, pepper, and garlic
4. Transfer the scallops to your Grill and smoke for 30-40 minutes
5. Sprinkle zest over your scallops and serve warm!

Texas Flounder

Prep Time: 15 minutes / Cook Time 30-40 minutes/ Serves: 8

Ingredients:

- 1 whole flounder
- 1 halved lemon
- Ground black pepper as needed
- 2 tablespoons of chopped up fresh dill
- 1 tablespoon of olive oil

Directions:

1 Pre-heat your Grill to a temperature of 350 degrees Fahrenheit
2 Clean up and scale your fresh flounder, making sure to leave the head
3 Take a sharp knife and make 3-4 diagonal slits across the body that are big enough for lemon slices
4 Slice half of your lemon and place them into the slices
5 Rub the fish with a coating of olive oil
6 Squeeze another half of the lemon all over the fish
7 Season with some black pepper
8 Rub about 1 tablespoon of dill into the slits and insert the lemon slices firmly
9 Place the flounder on top of a large piece of aluminum foil and fold the sides all around the fish
10 Make sure that enough foil is left so that you can seal the fish in a packet
11 Place the fish in your Grill and throw a couple of handful of soaked wood chips into the coals
12 Let it smoke for about 10 minutes
13 Once done, seal up the foil and smoke it until it is fully done (flesh should easily flake off)
14 Remove the fish from your grill and garnish with some extra dill. Serve!

Stuffed Up Shrimp Tilapia

Prep Time: 15 minutes / Cook Time 30-40 minutes/ Serves: 8

Ingredients:

- 5 ounce of fresh, farmed tilapia fillets
- 2 tablespoon of extra virgin olive oil
- 1 and a 1/2 teaspoon of smoked paprika
- 1 and a 1/2 teaspoon of old Bay Seasoning

For Shrimp Stuffing

- 1 pound of cooked and deveined shrimp (tail off)
- 1 tablespoon of salted butter
- 1 cup of finely diced red onion
- 1 cup of Italian bread crumbs
- 1/2 a cup of Italian bread crumbs
- 1/2 a cup of mayonnaise
- 1 beaten large eggs
- 2 teaspoon of freshly chopped parsley
- 1 and a 1/2 teaspoon of salt and pepper

Directions:

1 Take a food processor and add shrimp, chop them up
2 Take a skillet and place it over medium-high heat, add butter and allow it to melt
3 Sauté the onions for 3 minutes
4 Add chopped shrimp with cooled Sautéed onion alongside remaining ingredients listed under stuffing ingredients and transfer to a bowl
5 Cover the mixture and allow it to refrigerate for 60 minutes
6 Rub both sides of the fillet with olive oil
7 Spoon 1/3 cup of the stuffing to the fillet
8 Flatten out the stuffing onto the bottom half of the fillet and fold the Tilapia in half
9 Secure with 2 toothpicks
10 Dust each fillet with smoked paprika and Old Bay seasoning
11 Pre-heat your Grill to 400 degrees Fahrenheit
12 Add your preferred wood chips and transfer the fillets to a non-stick grill tray
13 Transfer to your Grill and Grill for 30-45 minutes until the internal temperature reaches 145 degrees Fahrenheit
14 Allow the fish to rest for 5 minutes and enjoy!

Chapter 4: Vegan & Vegeatarian Recipes

Smoked Mushrooms

Prep time: 15 minutes, Cook time: 45 minutes; Serves: 5

Ingredients

- 4 cup portobello, whole and cleaned
- 1 tbsp canola oil
- 1 tbsp onion powder
- 1 tbsp granulated garlic
- 1tbsp salt
- 1 tbsp pepper

Preparation Method

1. In a mixing bowl, add all the ingredients and mix well.
2. Set the Smoker temperature to 180°F then place the mushrooms directly on the grill.
3. Smoke the mushrooms for 30 minutes.
4. Increase the temperature to high and cook the mushrooms for a further 15 minutes.
5. Serve and enjoy.

grilled Zucchini Squash Spears

Prep time: 5 minutes, Cook time: 10 minutes; Serves: 5

Ingredients

- 4 zucchini, cleaned and ends cut
- 2 tbsp olive oil
- 1 tbsp sherry vinegar
- 2 thyme, leaves pulled
- Salt and pepper to taste

Preparation Method

1. Cut the zucchini into halves then cut each half thirds.
2. Add the rest of the ingredients in a ziplock bag with the zucchini pieces. Toss to mix well.
3. Preheat the Smoker temperature to 350°F with the lid closed for 15 minutes.
4. Remove the zucchini from the bag and place them on the grill grate with the cut side down.
5. Cook for 4 minutes per side or until the zucchini are tender.
6. Remove from grill and serve with thyme leaves. Enjoy.

Whole Roasted Cauliflower with Garlic Parmesan Butter

Prep time: 15 minutes, Cook time: 45 minutes; Serves: 5

Ingredients

- 1/4 cup olive oil
- Salt and pepper to taste
- 1 cauliflower, fresh
- 1/2 cup butter, melted
- 1/4 cup parmesan cheese, grated
- 2 garlic cloves, minced
- 1/2 tbsp parsley, chopped

Preparation Method

1. Preheat the grill with the lid closed for 15 minutes.
2. Meanwhile, brush the cauliflower with oil then season with salt and pepper.

3. Place the cauliflower in a cast iron and place it on a grill grate.
4. Cook for 45 minutes or until the cauliflower is golden brown and tender.
5. Meanwhile, mix butter, cheese, garlic, and parsley in a mixing bowl.
6. In the last 20 minutes of cooking, add the butter mixture.
7. Remove the cauliflower from the grill and top with more cheese and parsley if you desire. Enjoy.

Smoked Cold Smoked Cheese

Prep time: 5 minutes, Cook time: 2 minutes; Serves: 10

Ingredients
- Ice
- 1 aluminum pan, full-size and disposable
- 1 aluminum pan, half-size and disposable
- Toothpicks
- A block of cheese

Preparation Method
1. Preheat the Smoker to 165°F wit the lid closed for 15 minutes.
2. Place the small pan in the large pan. Fill the surrounding of the small pan with ice.
3. Place the cheese in the small pan on top of toothpicks then place the pan on the grill and close the lid.
4. Smoke cheese for 1 hour, flip the cheese, and smoke for 1 more hour with the lid closed.
5. Remove the cheese from the grill and wrap it in parchment paper. Store in the fridge for 2 3 days for the smoke flavor to mellow.
6. Remove from the fridge and serve.Enjoy.

grilled Asparagus and Honey Glazed Carrots

Prep time: 15 minutes, Cook time: 35 minutes; Serves: 5

Ingredients
- 1 bunch asparagus, trimmed ends
- 1 lb carrots, peeled
- 2 tbsp olive oil
- Sea salt to taste
- 2 tbsp honey
- Lemon zest

Preparation Method
1. Sprinkle the asparagus with oil and sea salt. Drizzle the carrots with honey and salt.
2. Preheat the Smoker to 165°F wit the lid closed for 15 minutes.
3. Place the carrots in the Smoker and cook for 15 minutes. Add asparagus and cook for 20 more minutes or until cooked through.
4. Top the carrots and asparagus with lemon zest. Enjoy.

Smoked Deviled Eggs

Prep time: 15 minutes, Cook time: 30 minutes; Serves: 5

Ingredients
- 7 hard-boiled eggs, peeled
- 3 tbsp mayonnaise
- 3 tbsp chives, diced
- 1 tbsp brown mustard
- 1 tbsp apple cider vinegar
- Dash of hot sauce
- Salt and pepper
- 2 tbsp cooked bacon, crumbled
- Paprika to taste

Preparation Method
1. Preheat the Smoker to 180°F for 15 minutes with the lid closed.
2. Place the eggs on the grill grate and

smoke the eggs for 30 minutes. Remove the eggs from the grill and let cool.
3. Half the eggs and scoop the egg yolks into a zip lock bag.
4. Add all other ingredients in the zip lock bag except bacon and paprika. Mix until smooth.
5. Pipe the mixture into the egg whites then top with bacon and paprika.
6. Let rest then serve and enjoy.

grilled Vegetables

Prep time: 5 minutes, Cook time: 15 minutes; Serves: 8

Ingredients

- 1 veggie tray
- 1/4 cup vegetable oil
- 2 tbsp veggie seasoning

Preparation Method

1. Preheat the grill to 375°F
2. Toss the vegetables in oil then place on a sheet pan.
3. Sprinkle with veggie seasoning then place on the hot grill.
4. Grill for 15 minutes or until the veggies are cooked.
5. Let rest then serve. Enjoy.

Smoked Asparagus

Prep time: 5 minutes, Cook time: 1 hour; Serves: 4

Ingredients

- 1 bunch fresh asparagus, ends cut
- 2 tbsp olive oil
- Salt and pepper to taste

Preparation Method

1. Fire up your Smokerto 230°F
2. Place the asparagus in a mixing bowl and drizzle with olive oil. Season with salt and pepper.
3. Place the asparagus in a tinfoil sheet and fold the sides such that you create a basket.
4. Smoke the asparagus for 1 hour or until soft turning after half an hour.
5. Remove from the grill and serve. Enjoy.

Smoked Acorn Squash

Prep time: 10 minutes, Cook time: 2 hours; Serves: 6

Ingredients

- 3 tbsp olive oil
- 3 acorn squash, halved and seeded
- 1/4 cup unsalted butter
- 1/4 cup brown sugar
- 1 tbsp cinnamon, ground
- 1 tbsp chili powder
- 1 tbsp nutmeg, ground

Preparation Method

1. Brush olive oil on the acorn squash cut sides then cover the halves with foil. Poke holes on the foil to allow steam and smoke through.
2. Fire up the Smoker to 225°F and smoke the squash for 1-1/2-2 hours.
3. Remove the squash from the smoker and allow it to sit.
4. Meanwhile, melt butter, sugar and spices in a saucepan. Stir well to combine.
5. Remove the foil from the squash and spoon the butter mixture in each squash half. Enjoy.

Vegan Smoked Carrot Dogs

Prep time: 25 minutes, Cook time: 35 minutes; Serves: 4

Ingredients

- 4 thick carrots
- 2 tbsp avocado oil
- 1 tbsp liquid smoke
- 1/2 tbsp garlic powder
- Salt and pepper to taste

1. Preheat the grill to 425°F and line a baking sheet with parchment paper.
2. Peel the carrots and round the edges.
3. In a mixing bowl, mix oil, liquid smoke, garlic, salt, and pepper. Place the carrots on the baking dish then pour the mixture over.
4. Roll the carrots to coat evenly with the mixture and use fingertips to massage the mixture into the carrots.
5. Place in the grill and grill for 35 minutes or until the carrots are fork-tender ensuring to turn and brush the carrots every 5 minutes with the marinade.
6. Remove from the grill and place the carrots in hot dog bun. Serve with your favorite toppings and enjoy.

Grill Spicy Sweet Potatoes

Prep time: 10 minutes, Cook time: 35 minutes; Serves: 6

Ingredients

- 2 lb sweet potatoes, cut into chunks
- 1 red onion, chopped
- 2 tbsp oil
- 2 tbsp orange juice
- 1 tbsp roasted cinnamon
- 1 tbsp salt
- 1/4 tbsp Chiptole chili pepper

Preparation Method

1. Preheat the grill to 425°F with the lid closed.
2. Toss the sweet potatoes with onion, oil, and juice.

3. In a mixing bowl, mix cinnamon, salt, and pepper then sprinkle the mixture over the sweet potatoes.
4. Spread the potatoes on a lined baking dish in a single layer.
5. Place the baking dish in the grill and grill for 30 minutes or until the sweet potatoes ate tender.
6. Serve and enjoy.

grilled Stuffed Zucchini

Prep time: 5 minutes, Cook time: 11 minutes; Serves: 8

Ingredients

- 4 zucchini
- 5 tbsp olive oil
- 2 tbsp red onion, chopped
- 1/4 tbsp garlic, minced
- 1/2 cup bread crumbs
- 1/2 cup mozzarella cheese, shredded
- 1 tbsp fresh mint
- 1/2 tbsp salt
- 3 tbsp parmesan cheese

Preparation Method

1. Cut the zucchini lengthwise and scoop out the pulp then brush the shells with oil.
2. In a non-stick skillet sauté pulp, onion, and remaining oil. Add garlic and cook for a minute.
3. Add bread crumbs and cook until golden brown. Remove from heat and stir in mozzarella cheese, fresh mint, and salt.
4. Spoon the mixture into the shells and sprinkle parmesan cheese.
5. Place in a grill and grill for 10 minutes or until the zucchini are tender.

grilled Mexican Street Corn

Prep time: 5 minutes, Cook time: 25 minutes;

Serves: 6

Ingredients

- 6 ears of corn on the cob, shucked
- 1 tbsp olive oil
- Kosher salt and pepper to taste
- 1/4 cup mayo
- 1/4 cup sour cream
- 1 tbsp garlic paste
- 1/2 tbsp chili powder
- Pinch of ground red pepper
- 1/2 cup cotija cheese, crumbled
- 1/4 cup cilantro, chopped
- 6 lime wedges

Preparation Method

1. Brush the corn with oil and sprinkle with salt.
2. Place the corn on a grill set at 350°F. Cook for 25 minutes as you turn it occasionally.
3. Meanwhile mix mayo, cream, garlic, chili, and red pepper until well combined.
4. When the corn is cooked remove from the grill, let it rest for some minutes then brush with the mayo mixture.
5. Sprinkle cotija cheese, more chili powder, and cilantro. Serve with lime wedges. Enjoy.

Grilled Bacon Wrapped Jalapeno Poppers

Prep time: 10 minutes, Cook time: 20 minutes; Serves: 6

Ingredients

- 6 jalapenos, fresh
- 4 oz cream cheese
- 1/2 cup cheddar cheese, shredded
- 1 tbsp vegetable rub
- 12 slices cut bacon

Preparation Method

1. Preheat the Smokerand grill to375°F.
2. Slice the jalapenos lengthwise and scrape the seed and membrane. Rinse them with water and set aside.
3. In a mixing bowl, mix cream cheese, cheddar cheese, vegetable rub until well mixed.
4. Fill the jalapeno halves with the mixture then wrap with the bacon pieces.
5. Smoke for 20 minutes or until the bacon crispy.
6. Serve and enjoy.

Smoked Mushrooms

This will make the most flavorful mushroom you will ever have. It is smoked in a Grill and given the smoky savory flavor. You will love it. Prep time: 15 minutes, Cook time: 45 minutes; Serves 2

Ingredients

- 4 cups whole baby portobello, cleaned
- 1 tbsp canola oil
- 1 tbsp onion powder
- 1 tbsp garlic, granulated
- 1 tbsp salt
- 1 tbsp pepper

Preparation Method

1. Place all the ingredients in a bowl, mix, and combine.
2. Set your Grill to 180°F.
3. Place the mushrooms on the grill directly and smoke for about 30 minutes.
4. Increase heat to high and cook the mushroom for another 15 minutes.
5. Serve warm and enjoy!

Grilled Zucchini Squash Spears

Prep time: 5 minutes, Cook time: 10 minutes; Serves 4

Ingredients

- 4 zucchini, medium
- 2 tbsp olive oil
- 1 tbsp sherry vinegar
- 2 thyme, leaves pulled
- Salt to taste
- Pepper to taste

Preparation Method

1. Clean zucchini, cut ends off, half each lengthwise, and cut each half into thirds.
2. Combine all the other ingredients in a zip lock bag, medium, then add spears.
3. Toss well and mix to coat the zucchini.
4. Preheat Grill to 350°F with the lid closed for about 15 minutes.
5. Remove spears from the zip lock bag and place them directly on your grill grate with the cut side down.
6. Cook for about 3-4 minutes until zucchini is tender and grill marks show.
7. Remove them from the grill and enjoy.

Grilled Asparagus & Honey-Glazed Carrots

Prep time: 15 minutes, Cook time: 35 minutes; Serves 4

Ingredients

- 1 bunch asparagus, woody ends removed
- 2 tbsp olive oil
- 1 lb peeled carrots
- 2 tbsp honey
- Sea salt to taste
- Lemon zest to taste

Preparation Method

1. Rinse the vegetables under cold water.
2. Splash the asparagus with oil and generously with a splash of salt.
3. Drizzle carrots generously with honey and splash lightly with salt.

4. Preheat your Grill to 350°F with the lid closed for about 15 minutes.
5. Place the carrots first on the grill and cook for about 10-15 minutes.
6. Now place asparagus on the grill and cook both for about 15-20 minutes or until done to your liking.
7. Top with lemon zest and enjoy.

Grilled Vegetables

Prep time: 5 minutes, Cook time: 15 minutes; Serves 12

Ingredients

- 1 veggie tray
- 1/4 cup vegetable oil
- 1-2 tbsp Traeger veggie seasoning

Preparation Method

1. Preheat your Grill to 375°F.
2. Meanwhile, toss the veggies in oil placed on a sheet pan, large, then splash with the seasoning.
3. Place on the Grill and grill for about 10-15 minutes.
4. Remove, serve, and enjoy.

Smoked Acorn Squash

Prep time: 10 minutes, Cook time: 2 hours; Serves 6

Ingredients

- 3 acorn squash, seeded and halved
- 3 tbsp olive oil
- 1/4 cup butter, unsalted
- 1 tbsp cinnamon, ground
- 1 tbsp chili powder
- 1 tbsp nutmeg, ground
- 1/4 cup brown sugar

Preparation Method

1. Brush the cut sides of your squash with olive oil then cover with foil poking holes

for smoke and steam to get through.
2. Preheat your Grill to 225°F.
3. Place the squash halves on the grill with the cut side down and smoke for about 1½- 2 hours. Remove from the Grill.
4. Let it sit while you prepare spiced butter. Melt butter in a saucepan then add spices and sugar stirring to combine.
5. Remove the foil form the squash halves.
6. Place 1 tbsp of the butter mixture onto each half. Serve and enjoy!

Vegan Smoked Carrot Dogs

Prep time: 10 minutes, Cook time: 35 minutes; Serves 2

Ingredients

- 4 carrots, thick
- 2 tbsp avocado oil
- 1/2 tbsp garlic powder
- 1 tbsp liquid smoke
- Pepper to taste
- Kosher salt to taste

Preparation Method

1. Preheat your Grill to 425°F then line a parchment paper on a baking sheet.
2. Peel the carrots to resemble a hot dog. Round the edges when peeling.
3. Whisk together oil, garlic powder, liquid smoke, pepper and salt in a bowl, small.
4. Now place carrots on the baking sheet and pour the mixture over. Roll your carrots in the mixture to massage seasoning and oil into them. Use fingertips.
5. Roast the carrots in the Grill until fork tender for about 35 minutes. Brush the carrots using the marinade mixture every 5 minutes.
6. Remove and place into hot dog buns then top with hot dog toppings of your choice.

7. Serve and enjoy!

Easy Smoked Vegetables

Prep time: 15 minutes, Cook time: 15 minutes; Serves 6

Ingredients

- 1 ear fresh corn, silk and husks strands removed
- 1 yellow squash, medium and 1/2 inch slices
- 1 red onion, small and cut to thin wedges
- 1 green bell pepper, small and 1-inch strips
- 1 red bell pepper, small and 1-inch strips
- 1 yellow bell pepper, small and 1-inch strips
- 1 cup halved mushrooms
- 2 tbsp vegetable oil
- 2 tbsp seasoning

Preparation Method

1. Preheat your Grill on high heat with the lid open for about 10 minutes until smoke appears. Now reduce to medium heat.
2. In the meantime, toss vegetables in a bowl, large, with oil then splash with seasoning. Toss to coat everything well.
3. Place the vegetable on the grill rack.
4. Smoke for about 10-12 minutes over medium heat until tender. Turn occasionally.
5. Serve warm.

Stuffed Grilled Zucchini

Prep time: 25 minutes, Cook time: 10 minutes; Serves 4

Ingredients

- 4 zucchini, medium
- 5 tbsp olive oil, divided
- 2 tbsp red onion, finely chopped

- 1/4 tbsp garlic, minced
- 1/2 cup bread crumbs, dry
- 1/2 cup shredded mozzarella cheese, part-skim
- 1/2 tbsp salt
- 1 tbsp fresh mint, minced
- 3 tbsp parmesan cheese, grated

Preparation Method

1. Halve zucchini lengthwise and scoop pulp ou. Leave 1/4 -inch shell. Now brush using 2 tbsp oil, set aside, and chop the pulp.
2. Saute onion and pulp in a skillet, large, then add garlic and cook for about 1 minute.
3. Add bread crumbs and cook while stirring for about 2 minutes until golden brown.
4. Remove everything from heat then stir in mozzarella cheese, salt, and mint. Scoop into the zucchini shells and splash with parmesan cheese.
5. Preheat your Grill to 375°F.
6. Place stuffed zucchini on the Grill while covered for about 8-10 minutes until tender.
7. Serve warm and enjoy.

Smoked Stuffed Mushrooms

Prep time: 15 minutes, Cook time: 1 hour 15 minutes; Serves 12

Ingredients

- 12-16 white mushrooms, large, cleaned and stems removed
- 1/2 cup parmesan cheese
- 1/2 cup bread crumbs, Italian
- 2 minced garlic cloves
- 2 tbsp fresh parsley, chopped
- 1/4 -1/3 cup olive oil
- Salt and pepper to taste

Preparation Method

1. Preheat your Grill 375°F.
2. Remove mushroom very bottom stem then dice the rest into small pieces.
3. Combine mushroom stems, parmesan cheese, bread crumbs, garlic, parsley, 3 tbsp oil, pepper, and salt in a bowl, large. Combine until moist.
4. Layer mushrooms in a pan, disposable, then fill them with the mixture until heaping. Drizzle with more oil.
5. Place the pan on the Grill.
6. Smoke for about 1 hour 20 minutes until filling browns and mushrooms become tender.
7. Remove from Grill and serve.
8. Enjoy!

Bacon-Wrapped Jalapeno Poppers

Prep time: 10 minutes, Cook time: 20 minutes; Serves 6

Ingredients

- 6 jalapenos, Fresh
- 1/2 cup shredded cheddar cheese
- 4 oz soft cream cheese
- 1-1/2 tbsp Traeger veggie rub
- 12 bacon slices, thin cut

Preparation Method

1. Preheat your Grill to 375°F.
2. Halve the jalapenos lengthwise then scrape membrane and seeds using a spoon. rinse them and set aside.
3. Meanwhile, combine cheddar cheese, cream cheese, and veggie rub in a bowl, medium stirring until incorporated fully.
4. Fill the jalapenos with your cheese mixture then wrap each half with a bacon slice.
5. Place on your grill and grill for about 15-

20 minutes until bacon becomes crispy and peppers are soft.

6. Serve and enjoy.

Herbed Cauliflower

Prep Time: 20 minutes/ Cook Time 2 hours / Serves: 4

Ingredients:

- 1 cauliflower head
- Salt and pepper to taste
- Olive oil
- 2 teaspoons dried oregano
- 2 teaspoons dried basil

Directions:

1. Pre-heat your Grill to 200 degrees F
2. Take cauliflower and chop into medium-sized pieces, remove the core
3. Transfer pieces of cauliflower onto a sheet pan and drizzle olive oil
4. Sprinkle seasoning and herbs over cauliflower, transfer to Grill
5. Smoke for 2 hours
6. Serve and enjoy!

Portobello Mushrooms

Prep Time: 20 minutes/ Cook Time 2 hours / Serves: 4

Ingredients:

- 12 large Portobello mushrooms
- 1 tablespoon Herbs de Provence
- 1/4 cup extra virgin olive oil
- Salt and pepper to taste

Directions:

1. Pre-heat your Grill to 200 degrees F
2. Take a bowl and mix in Herbs de Provence, olive oil, salt, and pepper
3. Clean mushrooms using a dry cloth
4. Rub mushrooms al over with herbs

mixture, transfer mushrooms, cap side down on top grill rack

5. Smoke for 2 hours
6. Remove carefully and serve, enjoy!

Smoked Tomato And Mozzarella Dip

Prep Time: 20 minutes/ Cook Time 60 minutes / Serves: 4

Ingredients:

- 8 ounces smoked mozzarella cheese, shredded
- 8 ounces Colby cheese, shredded
- 1/2 cup parmesan cheese, grated
- 1 cup sour cream
- 1 cup sun-dried tomatoes
- 1 and 1/2 teaspoon salt
- 1 teaspoon pepper
- 1 teaspoon dried basil
- 1 teaspoon dried oregano
- 1 teaspoon red pepper flakes
- 1 garlic clove, minced
- 1/2 teaspoon onion powder
- Fresh toast for serving

Directions:

1. Pre-heat your Grill to 275 degrees F
2. Take a large bowl and stir in cheese, tomatoes, pepper, salt, basil, oregano, pepper flakes, garlic, onion powder and mix well
3. Transfer mix to a hard steel skillet and transfer to your Grill
4. Smoke for 1 hour
5. Serve and enjoy!

Smoked Potatoes

Prep Time: 20 minutes/ Cook Time 3 hours / Serves: 4

Ingredients:

- 2 russet potatoes
- 3/4 cup sour cream
- 1 cup cheddar cheese
- 2 tablespoons green onion
- 8 bacon strips
- 4 tablespoons butter
- 2 tablespoons olive oil
- Salt as needed

Directions:

1. Pre-heat your Grill to 200 degrees F
2. Take oil and salt, rub on potatoes and wrap potatoes in foil
3. Transfer to Grill
4. Smoke for 3 hours, cut off the top each potato and remove potato flesh, leave shell empty
5. Fry and crumble the bacon, add potato flesh with bacon, butter, sour cream, cheese in a bowl
6. Add prepared filling into the potatoes, add cheese on top
7. Wrap potato with 2 bacon slices, secure with a toothpick
8. Smoke for 1 hour more
9. Add green onions with little sour cream, on top
10. Serve and enjoy!

Fine Grilled Cabbage

Prep Time: 20 minutes/ Cook Time 2 hours / Serves: 4

Ingredients:

- 1 head of cabbage, cored completely
- 4 tablespoon of butter
- 2 tablespoon of rendered bacon fat
- 1 chicken bouillon cube
- 1 teaspoon of freshly ground black pepper
- 1 minced garlic clove

Directions:

1. Pre-heat your Grill to 240 degrees F
2. Core cabbage and add butter, cube, bacon fat, pepper and garlic to the hole
3. Wrap cabbage in foil about 2/3rds way up
4. Keep the top open
5. Transfer to Egg and smoke for 2 hours
6. Enjoy!

Garlic And Rosemary Potato Wedges

Prep Time: 20 minutes/ Cook Time 2 hours / Serves: 4

Ingredients:

- 4-6 large russet potatoes, cut up into wedges
- 1/4 cup of olive oil
- 2 minced garlic cloves
- 2 tablespoon of chopped rosemary leaves
- 2 teaspoon of salt
- 1 teaspoon of freshly ground black pepper
- 1 teaspoon of sugar
- 1 teaspoon of onion powder

Directions:

1. Pre-heat your Grill to 250 degrees F
2. Take a large bowl and add potatoes and olive oil, mix well
3. Take another small bowl and add garlic, salt, rosemary, pepper, sugar, onion powder and sprinkle on all sides of the wedges
4. Transfer to a rack and your Grill
5. Smoke for 1 and 1/2 hours Enjoy!

Smoked Mac And Cheese

Prep Time: 20 minutes/ Cook Time 60 minutes / Serves: 4

Ingredients:

- 4 tablespoons butter
- 3 tablespoons all-purpose flour
- 3 cups whole milk
- 2 cups cheddar cheese, shredded
- 2 cups jack cheese, shredded
- 1 cup parmesan cheese, grated
- 8 ounces cream cheese, cubed
- 2 teaspoons salt
- 1 teaspoon fresh ground black pepper
- 1 pound elbow macaroni, cooked
- Cooking spray to taste

Directions:

1. Pre-heat your Grill to 225 degrees F
2. Take a large saucepan and place it over medium heat, add butter and let it heat p
3. Whisk in flour and whisk for 1 minute, slowly whisk in milk and bring the mix to a boil. Lower heat to low and simmer for 5 minutes, remove heat
4. Add cheese and stir until cheese melts
5. Stir in pepper, salt, and cooked macaroni
6. Spray an aluminum foil roasting pan with cooking spray and transfer the mac and cheese mix
7. Top with remaining cheese. Smoke for 1 hour until bubbly Enjoy!

Fired Up Artichokes

Prep Time: 10 minutes/ Cook Time 120 minutes / Serves: 4

Ingredients:

- 1/2 a cup of olive oil
- 1 minced garlic clove
- 1 teaspoon of salt
- Juice of 1 lemon
- 4 artichokes, stemmed and halve lengthwise

Directions:

1. Pre-heat your Grill to 225 degrees Fahrenheit using your preferred wood chips
2. Take a small bowl and whisk in olive oil, salt, lemon juice and garlic
3. Brush the artichoke halves with season olive oil
4. Transfer them to your Grill and smoke for 2 hours
5. Enjoy!

Smoked Tomato And Mozzarella Dip

Prep Time: 10 minutes/ Cook Time 60 minutes / Serves: 4

Ingredients:

- 8 ounce of smoked mozzarella cheese, shredded
- 8 ounce of shredded Colby cheese
- 1/2 a cup of grated Parmesan cheese
- 1 cup of sour cream
- 1 cup of sun-dried tomatoes
- 1 and a 1/2 teaspoon of salt
- 1 teaspoon of freshly ground black pepper
- 1 teaspoon of dried basil
- 1 teaspoon of dried oregano
- 1 teaspoon of red pepper flakes
- 1 garlic clove finely, minced
- 1/2 a teaspoon of onion powder
- French toast for serving

Directions:

1. Pre-heat your Grill to 275 degrees Fahrenheit
2. Take a large bowl and stir in the cheeses, tomatoes, pepper, salt, basil, oregano, red pepper flakes, garlic, onion powder

and mix well

3. Transfer the mix to a small metal pan and transfer to Grill

4. Smoke for 1 hour
5. Serve with toasted French bread
6. Enjoy!

Chapter 5: Appetizers and Side Dishes

Grilled Carrots

Prep time: 5 minutes, Cook time: 20 minutes;
Serves 6

Ingredients

- 1 lb carrots, large
- 1/2 tbsp salt
- 6 oz butter
- 1/2 tbsp black pepper
- Fresh thyme

Preparation Method

1. Thoroughly wash the carrots and do not peel. Pat them dry and coat with olive oil.
2. Add salt to your carrots.
3. Meanwhile, preheat a Grill to 350°F.
4. Now place your carrots directly on the grill or on a raised rack.
5. Close and cook for about 20 minutes.
6. While carrots cook, cook butter in a saucepan, small, over medium heat until browned. Stir constantly to avoid it from burning. Remove from heat.
7. Remove carrots from the grill onto a plate then drizzle with browned butter.
8. Add pepper and splash with thyme.
9. Serve and enjoy.

Grilled Brussels Sprouts

Prep time: 15 minutes, Cook time: 20 minutes;
Serves 8

Ingredients

- 1/2 lb bacon, grease reserved
- 1 lb Brussels Sprouts
- 1/2 tbsp pepper
- 1/2 tbsp salt

Preparation Method

1. Cook bacon until crispy on a stovetop, reserve its grease then chop into small pieces.
2. Meanwhile, wash the Brussels sprouts, trim off the dry end and remove dried leaves if any. Half them and set aside.
3. Place 1/4 cup reserved grease in a pan, cast-iron, over medium-high heat.
4. Season the Brussels sprouts with pepper and salt.
5. Brown the sprouts on the pan with the cut side down for about 3-4 minutes.
6. In the meantime, preheat your Grill to 350-375°F.
7. Place bacon pieces and browned sprouts into your grill-safe pan.
8. Cook for about 20 minutes.
9. Serve immediately.

Grilled Spicy Brisket

Prep time: 20 minutes, Cook time: 9 hours;
Serves: 10

Ingredients

- 2 tbsp garlic powder
- 2 tbsp onion powder
- 2 tbsp paprika
- 2 tbsp chili powder
- 1/3 cup salt
- 1/3 cup black pepper
- 12 lb whole packer brisket, trimmed
- 1-1/2 cup beef broth

Preparation Method

1. Set your Smoker temperature to 225°F. Let preheat for 15 minutes with the lid closed.

2. Meanwhile, mix garlic, onion, paprika, chili, salt, and pepper in a mixing bowl.
1. the brisket generously on all sides.

Hickory Smoked Green Beans

Prep time: 15 minutes, Cook time: 3 hours; Serves 10

Ingredients

- 6 cups fresh green beans, halved and ends cut off
- 2 cups chicken broth
- 1 tbsp pepper, ground
- 1/4 tbsp salt
- 2 tbsp apple cider vinegar
- 1/4 cup diced onion
- 6-8 bite-size bacon slices
- **Optional:** sliced almonds

Preparation Method

1. Add green beans to a colander then rinse well. Set aside.
2. Place chicken broth, pepper, salt, and apple cider in a pan, large. Add green beans.
3. Blanch over medium heat for about 3-4 minutes then remove from heat.
4. Transfer the mixture into an aluminum pan, disposable. Make sure all mixture goes into the pan so do not drain them.
5. Place bacon slices over the beans and place the pan into the Smoker,
6. Smoke for about 3 hours uncovered.
7. Remove from the smoker and top with almonds slices.
8. Serve immediately.

Smoked Corn on the Cob

Prep time: 5 minutes, Cook time: 1 hour; Serves 4

Ingredients

- 4 corn ears, husk removed

- 4 tbsp olive oil
- Pepper and salt to taste

Preparation Method

1. Preheat your smoker to 225°F.
2. Meanwhile, brush your corn with olive oil. Season with pepper and salt.
3. Place the corn on a smoker and smoke for about 1 hour 15 minutes.
4. Remove from the smoker and serve.
5. Enjoy!

Smoked Vegetables

Prep time: 5 minutes, Cook time: 20 minutes; Serves 4

Ingredients

- 1 head of broccoli
- 4 carrots
- 16 oz snow peas
- 1 tbsp olive oil
- 1 cup mushrooms, chopped
- 1-1/2 tbsp pepper
- 1 tbsp garlic powder

Preparation Method

1. Cut broccoli and carrots into bite-size pieces. Add snow peas and combine.
2. Toss the veggies with oil and seasoning.
3. Now cover a pan, sheet, with parchment paper. Place veggies on top.
4. Meanwhile, set your Smoker to 180°F.
5. Place the pan into the smoker. Smoke for about 5 minutes.
6. Adjust smoker temperature to 400°F and continue cooking for another 10-15 minutes until slightly brown broccoli tips.
7. Remove, Serve and enjoy.

Easy Grilled Corn

Prep time: 5 minutes, Cook time: 40 minutes; Serves 6

Ingredients

- 6 fresh corn ears, still in the husk
- Pepper, salt and butter

Preparation Method

1. Preheat your grill to 375-400°F.
2. Cut off the large silk ball from the corn top and any hanging or loose husk pieces.
3. Place the corn on your grill grate directly and do not peel off the husk.
4. Grill for about 30-40 minutes. Flip a few times to grill evenly all round.
5. Transfer the corn on a platter, serve, and let guests peel their own.
6. Now top with pepper, salt and butter.
7. Enjoy!

Seasoned Potatoes on Smoker

Prep time: 10 minutes, Cook time: 45 minutes; Serves 6

Ingredients

- 1-1/2 lb creamer potatoes
- 2 tbsp olive oil
- 1 tbsp garlic powder
- 1/4 tbsp oregano
- 1/2 tbsp thyme, dried
- 1/2 tbsp parsley, dried

Preparation Method

1. Preheat your Grill to 350°F.
2. Spray an 8x8 inch foil pan using non-stick spray.
3. Mix all ingredients in the pan and place it into the grill.
4. Cook for about 45 minutes until potatoes are done. Stir after every 15 minutes.
5. Serve and enjoy!

Red Cabbage with Sultanas

Prep time: 24 hours 10 minutes| Cook time: 5 minutes| Serves: 2

Ingredients:

- Tbsp balsamic vinegar
- 1 small red cabbage, chopped into thin segments.
- 3.5oz Sultanas
- sunflower oil
- 3.5 oz soft brown sugar
- 7 Tbsp Riesling

Directions:

1. Soak sultanas in a bowl of Riesling for 24 hours. Preheat pan on the grid, add balsamic and sugar, then cook until sugar completely dissolves.
2. Place the cabbage in a large resealable bag and pour some marinade into it. Refrigerate bag for 24 hours.
3. Preheat Grill with Steel Grid and Plancha Griddle to 356°F.
4. Take out cabbage from marinade and keep the marinade. Oil the grid with sunflower oil and stir fry cabbage. Add one Tbsp of the marinade into the cabbage and stir.
5. Take out stirred-fried cabbage and serve with sultana.

Butter Beans and Water Cress Salad

Prep time: 10 minutes| Cook time: 8minutes| Serves: 2

Ingredients:

- 1 clove garlic, minced
- 10 green olives, minced
- 1/4 cup basil leaves, chopped
- 1/4 cup parsley leaves, chopped
- 1/4 bunch oregano leaves, chopped
- 1/2 bunch of watercress, chopped
- Olive oil

- 12 oz butter beans

Directions:

1. Preheat the EGG to 428°F
2. Blanch butter beans in salted water for 4 minutes, and then drain out water.
3. Mix the beans, olives, and garlic in a bowl. Place the mixture on the grid of the Grill and grill for 8 minutes.
4. Remove the stirred fried butter beans and place them in a bowl. Sprinkle pepper and salt. Garnish beans with fresh herbs and watercress, and then drizzle in olive oil.

Stir-Fried Noodles

Prep time: 15 minutes| Cook time: 5 minutes| Serves: 2

Ingredients:

- 1lb precooked udon noodles
- 2 shallots, cut into rings
- 1 sweet yellow pepper, seeded and chopped
- 1 red sweet pepper, seeded and chopped
- 1/2 Chinese cabbage
- 1 Tbsp oyster sauce
- 1 Tbsp black bean garlic sauce
- 2 Tbsp teriyaki sauce
- Shiitake mushroom, cut into slices
- 1 Tbsp ginger syrup
- 2 spring onions
- 1/2 red chili pepper

Directions:

1. Preheat Grill and Carbon Steel Grill wok in a basket to 428°F.
2. Mix the oyster sauce, garlic sauce, teriyaki sauce and ginger syrup in a small bowl.
3. Add shallots, mushroom, and pepper to the grill wok and stir fry for 2 minutes.
4. Stir in udon noodles and cook for 1 minute. Add chili pepper, cabbage, spring onions, and sauce. Stir noodles continuously while cooking for another one minute.
5. Serve noodles with grilled chicken and a sprinkle of coriander leaves.

Stir-fry Cardamom Fennel Scallop

Prep time: 12 hours 10 minutes| Cook time: 10 minutes| Serves: 4

Ingredients:

- 4 clove garlic, chopped
- 12 large sea scallops
- 1 Tbsp fennel seeds
- 2 dried chili, chopped
- 1 Tbsp cilantro, finely chopped (garnish)
- 2 Tbsp canola oil
- 1 Tbsp yellow mustard seeds
- 1/2 cups unsweetened coconut milk
- 1/4 cardamom seeds
- 1 head broccoli, cut into florets
- 1lb baby corn cut lengthwise
- 1/2 lb fresh snow peas, trimmed

Directions:

1. Grind cardamom, fennel, and mustard seeds in a spice grinder until smooth. Place spice blend in a bowl.
2. Mix in garlic and chives into the spice blend. Coat the scallops with the mixture and leave in the refrigerator overnight to marinate.
3. Heat oil in the stir fry pan on the preheated grid for a minute. Arrange scallop in the hot oil and sear for 2 minutes, until brown. Cover the lid of Grill after every action.
4. Add milk into the pan and bring scallop to a simmer for 2 minutes. Transfer scallop to a serving bowl and drizzle pan

sauce over scallop.

5. Heat oil in the pan and stir fry squash, broccoli, peas, and corn for 2 minutes. Remove from heat and serve with scallops.

Thai Prawns with Pineapple and Green beans

Prep time: 5 minutes| Cook time: 12 minutes| Serves: 4

Ingredients:

- 1/4 lb pineapple chunks
- 1/4 lb cherry tomatoes
- 1/4 lb green bean
- 2 Tbsp ginger, grated
- 1/2 lb raw king-sized prawn
- 1 bunch basil leaves
- 1 Tbsp olive oil
- 2 stalks lemongrass, outer part removed and finely chopped

Sauce

- 1 Tbsp fish sauce
- 1 Tbsp soft brown sugar
- Tbsp lime juice
- 2 Tbsp chicken stock

Directions:

1. In a small bowl, combine the sauce ingredients and mix well.
2. Heat oil in the Stir fry pan on the cooking grid for a minute. Sauté the lemongrass and ginger for 2 minutes. Stir in beans, pineapple, cherry tomatoes and stir fry for 5 minutes, until beans are tender.
3. Pour in prawns and sauce, and stir fry for another 3 minutes.
4. Remove pan from the grid and sprinkle basil leaves over the top.

Panzanella Salad

Prep time: 15 minutes| Cook time: 3 minutes| Serves: 4

Ingredients:

- 1/2 cup basil leaves, chopped
- 1 cup grape tomatoes, halved
- 1 cup bocconcini
- 1 Tsp Dijon mustard
- 1/4 cup red wine vinegar
- 1/4 cup plus 2 Tbsp olive oil
- 1 Tsp garlic, minced
- 2 cup heirloom tomatoes, diced
- 1 cup canned garbanzo beans, drained and rinsed
- 1 cup cucumber, peeled and diced
- 3 cups 1-inch cubes ciabatta bread
- Kosher salt
- Ground pepper

Directions:

1. Set the Grill with Cast Iron Grid and perforated grill wok for direct cooking. Preheat Grill to 400°F.
2. In a bowl, combine the bread and two tablespoons olive oil. Arrange bread cubes on the wok, regularly stir and grill for 3 minutes.
3. Remove bread cubes from wok and place on a rimmed sheet pan.
4. In a large bowl, mix the garbanzo beans, cucumber, basil, mozzarella beans, heirloom tomatoes, grape tomatoes, and toasted bread cubes.
5. In a small bowl, combine the mustard, 1/3 cup olive oil, garlic, and vinegar. Add salt and pepper to taste.
6. Pour the dressing over tomato salad and serve.

Smoked Peaches

Prep Time: 20 minutes/ Cook Time 20-30 minutes / Serves: 4

Ingredients:

- fresh peaches

Directions:

1. Pre-heat your Grill to 200 degrees F
2. Transfer peaches directly onto your Grill and smoke for 30 minutes, the first 20 minutes should be skin side down while the final 10 should be skin side up
3. Remove from Grill and serve, enjoy!

Jalapeno Poppers

Prep Time: 20 minutes/ Cook Time 60 minutes / Serves: 4

Ingredients:

- 12 jalapeno peppers
- ounces cream cheese
- 4 ounces cheddar cheese
- 4 ounces mozzarella cheese
- 2 bread heel slices
- 12 bacon slices

Directions:

1. Pre-heat your Grill to 200 degrees F
2. Add all the cheese to your food processor and hit blend button, blend until smooth
3. Cut stems off the pepper and scoop out seeds, fill inside of pepper with cheese mix
4. Tear a small part of the bread from crusts and add into the end of your pepper, this ensures that the cheese does not come out oozing
5. Wrap pepper with bacon and secure with a tooth pick
6. Transfer to your Grill and smoke for 1 hour
7. Once done, enjoy it!

Feisty Almonds

Prep Time: 20 minutes/ Cook Time 60 minutes / Serves: 4

Ingredients:

- 3 tablespoon of melted butter
- 2 and a 1/2 a teaspoon of garlic powder
- 2 teaspoons of salt
- 1 teaspoon of freshly ground black pepper
- 1 teaspoon of onion powder
- 1 teaspoon of dried thyme
- 2 cups of raw almonds

Directions:

1. Pre-heat your Grill to 225 degrees Fahrenheit
2. Line a rimmed baking sheet with parchment paper and grease the paper with cooking spray
3. Take a medium bowl and add butter, garlic powder, onion powder, salt, pepper and thyme
4. Add almonds and stir
5. Arrange the almonds in a single layer in your baking pan and smoke for 1 hour, making sure to smoke once
6. Remove and allow them to cool
7. Dry overnight in an airtight container and serve as needed!

Stuffed Chorizo Peppers

Prep Time: 20 minutes/ Cook Time 120 minutes / Serves: 4

Ingredients:

- 3 cups of shredded cheese
- 2 pound of ground chorizo sausage
- 4 poblano peppers, halved lengthwise and seeded
- bacon slices (uncooked)

Directions:

1. Pre-heat your Grill to 225 degrees

Fahrenheit
2. Take a large bowl and add 2 cups of cheddar with sausage
3. Divide the mix into 8 portions and press one portion into each pepper half
4. Sprinkle rest of the cheddar on top
5. Wrap each pepper half with 1 bacon slice, making sure to tuck in the edges to secure it
6. Transfer peppers to your Grill and smoke for 2 hours until the internal temperature of the sausage reaches 165 degrees Fahrenheit
7. Enjoy!

Delicious Bologna

Prep Time: 10 minutes/ Cook Time 60 minutes / Serves: 4

Ingredients:

- 2 tablespoon of chili powder
- 2 tablespoons of packed brown sugar
- 1 teaspoon of ground coriander
- 1 teaspoon of ground nutmeg
- 1 teaspoon of garlic powder
- 5-pound all-beef bologna chub
- 1/4 cup of prepped yellow mustard
- Salt as needed
- Freshly ground black pepper

Directions:

1. Pre-heat your Grill to 250 degrees Fahrenheit
2. Take a small bowl and add chili powder, coriander, brown sugar, nutmeg, and garlic powder
3. Keep it on the side
4. Cut the bologna into 1/2 inch slices and make few small cuts all around the edges of the slices
5. Coat both sides with the mustard mix

6. Season with salt, pepper and spice mix
7. Transfer the slices to Grill and smoke for 60 minutes
8. Enjoy!

Superb Spicy Chipotle Wings

Prep Time: 10 minutes/ Cook Time 60-120 minutes /
Serves: 8

Ingredients:

- 2 tablespoon packed light brown sugar
- 1 and a 1/2 tablespoon of chipotle pepper
- 1 tablespoon of Hungarian smoked paprika
- 1 tablespoon of dry mustard
- 1 tablespoon of ground cumin
- 1 and a 1/2 teaspoon of salt
- and a 1/2 pound of chicken wings

Directions:

1. Take a small-sized bowl and add brown sugar, paprika, chipotle, mustard, salt and cumin
2. Transfer the chicken wings to a large resealable bag and pour the seasoning mix
3. Seal and shake the chicken
4. Refrigerate for 60 minutes
5. Pre-heat your Grill to 250 degrees Fahrenheit
6. Transfer the chicken to your Grill rack and smoke for 1 and a 1/2 to 2 hours
7. Check if the internal temperature is 165 degrees Fahrenheit and serve!

Plum Chicken Pops

Prep Time: 10 minutes/ Cook Time 60-120 minutes / Serves: 8

Ingredients:

- 12 chicken drumsticks
- 2 teaspoon of salt
- 2 teaspoon of fresh ground black pepper
- Plum sauce (homemade or store-bought)

Directions:

1. Pre-heat your Grill to 250-degree Fahrenheit
2. Stretch the skin away from drumsticks as much as possible Remove the tendons from each leg
3. Season the drumsticks with salt and pepper and transfer to your Grill rack
4. Smoker for 1 and a 1/2 hours
5. Baste the pops with plum sauce and transfer to Grill again, Grill for 30 minutes until the internal temperature reaches 165 degrees Fahrenheit
6. Allow them to rest for a while
7. Coat the meat with more sauce and enjoy!

Apple Pie

Prep Time: 20 minutes/ Cook Time 20-30 minutes / Serves: 4

Ingredients:

- apples
- 1/4 cup of sugar
- 1 tablespoon cornstarch
- Flour as needed
- 1 refrigerated pie crust
- 1/4 cup peach preserve

Directions:

1. Pre-heat your Grill to 275 degrees F
2. Take a medium-sized bowl and add apples, sugar, cornstarch and stir well until combined thoroughly
3. Transfer to one side
4. Dust a work surface with flour and roll out your pie crust

5. Transfer pie crust into the pie pan (no greasing)
6. Spread preserve on bottom of pan and top with apple slices
7. Transfer into Grill and smoke for 30-40 minutes
8. Serve and enjoy!

The Original Barbacoa

Prep Time: 20 minutes/ Cook Time 3 hours / Serves: 4

Ingredients:

- 1 and a 1/2 teaspoon of ground black pepper
- 1 tablespoon of dried oregano
- 1 and a 1/2 teaspoon of cayenne pepper
- 1 and a 1/2 teaspoon of chili powder
- 1/ and a 1/2 teaspoon of garlic powder
- 1 teaspoon of ground cumin
- 1 teaspoon of salt
- 3 pound of boneless beef chuck roast

Directions:

1. pre-heat to 200 degrees Fahrenheit
2. Take a small bowl and add oregano, cayenne pepper, black pepper, garlic powder, chili powder, cumin, salt, and seasoned salt
3. Mix well
4. Dip the chuck roast into your mixing bowl and rub the spice mix all over
5. Transfer the meat to your Grill and Grill for 1 and a 1/2 hours
6. Make sure to turn the meat after every 30 minutes, if you see less smoke formation, add more chips after every 30 minutes as well
7. Once the meat shows a dark red color with darkened edges, transfer the meat to a roasting pan and seal it tightly with

an aluminum foil

8. Preheat your oven to 325 degrees Fahrenheit
9. Transfer the meat to your oven and bake for 1 and a 1/2 hours more
10. Shred the meat using two forks and serve!

The Porky Onion Soup

Prep Time: 20 minutes/ Cook Time 4 hours / Serves: 4

Ingredients:

- A rack of pork spare ribs
- 2 packs of onion soup mix
- Barbecue pork rib rub (with salt, garlic powder, pepper, and paprika)
- 4 cups of water

Directions:

1. Remove the white membrane of the pork meat and trim off any excess fat
2. Pre-heat your Grill to 250 degrees Fahrenheit
3. Prepare your rub mixture by mixing salt, garlic powder, pepper and paprika in a bowl
4. Rub the rib with the mixture
5. Transfer to the Grill and Grill for 2 hours
6. Blend 2 packs of onion soup with 4 cups of water
7. Once smoking is complete, take a heavy aluminum foil and transfer the meat to the foil, pour the soup mix all over
8. Seal the ribs
9. Smoke for another 1 and a 1/2 hours
10. Gently open the foil and turn the rib, seal it up and smoke for 1 hour more
11. Slice and serve!

Chapter 6: Snacks and Desserts

Smoked Pumpkin Pie

Prep time: 10 minutes, Cook time: 50 minutes; Serves 8

Ingredients

- 1 tbsp cinnamon
- 1-1/2 tbsp pumpkin pie spice
- 15 oz can pumpkin
- 14 oz can sweetened condensed milk
- 2 beaten eggs
- 1 unbaked pie shell
- **Topping:** whipped cream

Preparation Method

1. Preheat your smoker to 325°F.
2. Place a baking sheet, rimmed, on the smoker upside down, or use a cake pan.
3. Combine all your ingredients in a bowl, large, except the pie shell then pour the mixture into a pie crust.
4. Place the pie on the baking sheet and smoke for about 50-60 minutes until a knife comes out clean when inserted. Make sure the center is set.
5. Remove and cool for about 2 hours or refrigerate overnight.
6. Serve with a whipped cream dollop and enjoy!

Smoked Nut Mix

Prep time: 15 minutes, Cook time: 20 minutes; Serves 8-12

Ingredients

- 3 cups mixed nuts (pecans, peanuts, almonds etc)
- 1/2 tbsp brown sugar
- 1 tbsp thyme, dried
- 1/4 tbsp mustard powder
- 1 tbsp olive oil, extra-virgin

Preparation Method

1. Preheat your Grill to 250°F with the lid closed for about 15 minutes.
2. Combine all ingredients in a bowl, large, then transfer into a cookie sheet lined with parchment paper.
3. Place the cookie sheet on a grill and grill for about 20 minutes.
4. Remove the nuts from the grill and let cool.
5. Serve and enjoy.

Grilled Peaches and Cream

Prep time: 15 minutes, Cook time: 8 minutes; Serves 8

Ingredients

- 4 halved and pitted peaches
- 1 tbsp vegetable oil
- 2 tbsp clover honey
- 1 cup cream cheese, soft with honey and nuts

Preparation Method

1. Preheat your Grill to medium-high heat.
2. Coat the peaches lightly with oil and place on the grill pit side down.
3. Grill for about 5 minutes until nice grill marks on the surfaces.
4. Turn over the peaches then drizzle with honey.
5. Spread and cream cheese dollop where the pit was and grill for additional 2-3 minutes until the filling becomes warm.

6. Serve immediately.

grill Chicken Flatbread

Prep time: 5 minutes, Cook time: 30 minutes; Serves 6

Ingredients

- 6 mini breads
- 1-1/2 cups divided buffalo sauce
- 4 cups cooked and cubed chicken breasts
- For drizzling: mozzarella cheese

Preparation Method

1. Preheat your Grill to 375 - 400°F.
2. Place the breads on a surface, flat, then evenly spread 1/2 cup buffalo sauce on all breads.
3. Toss together chicken breasts and 1 cup buffalo sauce then top over all the breads evenly.
4. Top each with mozzarella cheese.
5. Place the breads directly on the grill but over indirect heat. Close the lid.
6. Cook for about 5-7 minutes until slightly toasty edges, cheese is melted and fully hated chicken.
7. Remove and drizzle with ranch or blue cheese.
8. Enjoy!

Grilled Homemade Croutons

Prep time: 10 minutes, Cook time: 30 minutes; Serves 6

Ingredients

- 2 tbsp Mediterranean Blend Seasoning
- 1/4 cup olive oil
- 6 cups cubed bread

Preparation Method

1. Preheat your grill to 250°F.
2. Combine seasoning and oil in a bowl

then drizzle the mixture over the bread cubes. Toss to evenly coat.
3. Layer the bread cubes on a cookie sheet, large, and place on the grill.
4. Bake for about 30 minutes. Stir at intervals of 5 minutes for browning evenly.
5. Once dried out and golden brown, remove from the grill.
6. Serve and enjoy!

Smoked Cheddar Cheese

Prep time: 5 minutes, Cook time: 5 hour; Serves 2

Ingredients

- 2, 8-oz, cheddar cheese blocks

Preparation Method

1. Preheat and set your Grill to 90°F.
2. Place the cheese blocks directly on the grill grate and smoke for about 4 hours.
3. Remove and transfer into a plastic bag, resealable. Refrigerate for about 2 weeks to allow flavor from smoke to permeate your cheese.
4. Now enjoy!

Smoked Mac and Cheese

Prep time: 2 minutes, Cook time: 1 hour; Serves 8

Ingredients

- 1/2 cup butter, salted
- 1/3 cup flour
- 1/2 tbsp salt
- 6 cups whole milk
- Dash of Worcestershire
- 1/2 tbsp dry mustard
- 1 lb small cooked shells, al dente in well-salted water
- 2 cups white cheddar, smoked
- 2 cups cheddar jack cheese

- 1 cup crushed ritz

Preparation Method

1. Set your grill on "smoke" and run for about 5-10 minutes with the lid open until fire establishes. Now turn your grill to 325 °F then close the lid.
2. Melt butter in a saucepan, medium, over low--medium heat then whisk in flour.
3. Cook while whisking for about 5-6 minutes over low heat until light tan color.
4. Whisk in salt, milk, Worcestershire, and mustard over low-medium heat stirring frequently until a thickened sauce.
5. Stir noodles, small shells, white sauce, and 1 cup cheddar cheese in a large baking dish, 10x3" high-sided, coated with butter.
6. Top with 1 cup cheddar cheese and ritz.
7. Place on the grill and bake for about 25-30 minutes until a bubbly mixture and cheese melts.
8. Serve immediately. Enjoy!

Berry Cobbler on a Grill

Prep time: 15 minutes, Cook time: 35 minutes; Serves 8

Ingredients

For fruit filling
- 3 cups frozen mixed berries
- 1 lemon juice
- 1 cup brown sugar
- 1 tbsp vanilla extract
- 1 tbsp lemon zest, finely grated
- A pinch of salt

For cobbler topping
- 1-1/2 cups all-purpose flour
- 1-1/2 tbsp baking powder
- 3 tbsp sugar, granulated
- 1/2 tbsp salt
- 8 tbsp cold butter

- 1/2 cup sour cream
- 2 tbsp raw sugar

Preparation Method

1. Set your Grill on "smoke" for about 4-5 minutes with the lid open until fire establishes and your grill starts smoking.
2. Preheat your grill to 350 °F for about 10-15 minutes with the grill lid closed.
3. Meanwhile, combine frozen mixed berries, Lemon juice, brown sugar, vanilla, lemon zest and pinch of salt. Transfer into a skillet and let the fruit sit and thaw.
4. Mix flour, baking powder, sugar, and salt in a bowl, medium. Cut cold butter into peas sizes using a pastry blender then add to the mixture. Stir to mix everything together.
5. Stir in sour cream until dough starts coming together.
6. Pinch small pieces of dough and place over the fruit until fully covered. Splash the top with raw sugar.
7. Now place the skillet directly on the grill grate, close the lid and cook for about 35 minutes until juices bubble, and a golden-brown dough topping.
8. Remove the skillet from the Grill and cool for several minutes.
9. Scoop and serve warm.

Grill Apple Crisp

Prep time: 20 minutes, Cook time: 1 hour; Serves 15

Ingredients

Apples
- 10 large apples
- 1/2 cup flour
- 1 cup sugar, dark brown
- 1/2 tbsp cinnamon
- 1/2 cup butter slices

Crisp

- 3 cups oatmeal, old-fashioned
- 1-1/2 cups softened butter, salted
- 1-1/2 tbsp cinnamon
- 2 cups brown sugar

Preparation Method

1. Preheat your grill to 350 °F.
2. Wash, peel, core, and dice the apples into cubes, medium-size
3. Mix together flour, dark brown sugar, and cinnamon then toss with your apple cubes.
4. Spray a baking pan, 10x13", with cooking spray then place apples inside. Top with butter slices.
5. Mix all crisp ingredients in a medium bowl until well combined. Place the mixture over the apples.
6. Place on the grill and cook for about 1-hour checking after every 15-20 minutes to ensure cooking is even. Do not place it on the hottest grill part.
7. Remove and let sit for about 20-25 minutes
8. It's very warm.

Grilled Marinated Chicken Kabobs

Prep time: 45 minutes, Cook time: 12 minutes; Serves 6

Ingredients

Marinade
- 1/2 cup olive oi
- 2 tbsp white vinegar
- 1 tbsp lemon juice
- 1-1/2 tbsp salt
- 1/2 tbsp ground pepper
- 2 tbsp fresh chives, chopped
- 1-1/2 tbsp thyme, chopped
- 2 tbsp Italian parsley, chopped
- 1 tbsp minced garlic

Kabobs
- 1-1/2 lb chicken breast
- 12 crimini mushrooms
- 1 each orange, red and yellow bell pepper

Serve with
- Naan bread

Preparation Method

1. Mix all the marinade ingredients then toss the chicken and mushrooms until well coated.
2. Place in the fridge to marinate for 30 minutes.
3. Meanwhile, soak the skewers in water. And preheat your Grill to 450°F.
4. Assemble the kabobs and grill for 6 minutes on each side. Set aside.
5. Heat up the naan bread on the grill for 2 minutes .serve and enjoy.

Bacon-wrapped chicken tenders

Prep time: 25 minutes, Cook time: 30 minutes; Serves 6

Ingredients

- 1/2 tbsp Italian seasoning
- 1/2 tbsp salt
- 1/2 tbsp black pepper
- 1 tbsp paprika
- 1 tbsp garlic powder
- 1 tbsp onion powder
- 1lb chicken tenders
- 10 strips bacon
- 1/3 cup brown sugar
- 1 tbsp chili powder

Preparation Method

1. Preheat your Grill to 450°F.
2. In a small mixing bowl, mix seasoning, salt, pepper, paprika, garlic powder, and onion powder.

3. Sprinkle the mixture over all sides of the chicken tenders until well coated.
4. Wrap the bacon around the chicken tenders and tuck in the ends.
5. Mix sugar and chili powder in a bowl and sprinkle over the bacon-wrapped chicken.
6. Place the chicken on the grill and cook for 30 minutes or until chicken and bacon are cooked through.
7. Broil the chicken in a broiler for a few minutes to crisp up the bacon if you desire.
8. Serve and enjoy.

Smoked Italian Meatballs

Prep time: 15 minutes, Cook time: 1 hour 5 minutes; Serves 6

Ingredients

- 2 lb beef, ground
- 2 slices white bread
- 1/2 cup whole milk
- 1 tbsp salt
- 1/2 tbsp onion powder
- 1/2 tbsp minced garlic
- 2 tbsp Italian seasoning
- 1/4 tbsp black pepper

Preparation Method

1. In a mixing bowl, mix all the ingredients until well combined using your hands. Turn on your Grill and set it to smoke then line a baking sheet with parchment paper.
2. Roll golf size meatballs using your hands .and place them on the baking dish. Place the baking dish in the Grill and smoke for 35 minutes.
3. Increase the Grill heat to 325^0F and cook for 30 more minutes or until the internal temperature reaches 160^0F.
4. Serve when hot

Grilled Stuffed Burgers

Prep time: 20 minutes, Cook time: 15 minutes; Serves 6

Ingredients

- 3 lb ground beef
- 1/2 tbsp onion powder
- 1/4 tbsp garlic powder
- 1 tbsp salt
- 1/2 tbsp pepper
- 1-1/2 cups Colby jack cheese, shredded
- Johnny's seasoning salt
- 6 slices Colby Jack cheese

Preparation Method

1. Preheat your Grill to 375^0F.
2. Mix beef, onion powder, garlic powder, salt, and pepper until well combined. Make 12 patties.
3. Place cheese on the burger patty and cover with another patty then seal the edges.
4. Season with salt, then place the patties on the grill. Cook the patties on the grill grate for 8 minutes, flip the patties and cook for additional 5 minutes.
5. Place a slice of cheese on each patty and grill with the lid closed to melt the cheese.
6. Remove the patties from the Grill and let rest for 10 minutes. Serve and enjoy with a toasted bun.

Grilled Steak Kabobs

Prep time: 15 minutes, Cook time: 10 minutes; Serves 6

Ingredients

- 3 lb steak
- 2 small zucchini
- 1 onion
- 2 small yellow squash

- Salt and pepper
- 1 cup teriyaki sauce
- 3 tbsp sesame seeds, toasted

1. Preheat your Grill to 400^{0}F.
2. Cut the steak and veggies into skewable pieces.
3. Place the meat and veggies on the skewers then sprinkle with salt and pepper.
4. Place the skewers on the grill and cook for 5 minutes per side.
5. Remove the skewers, drizzle teriyaki sauce and top with sesame seeds.
6. Serve when hot. Enjoy.

Grilled Apple cake

Prep time: 15 minutes, Cook time: 45 minutes; Serves 12

Ingredients

Cake
- 1/2 cup canola oil
- 1-1/2 cup brown sugar
- 1 egg
- 1 cup sour cream
- 1 tbsp baking soda
- 1/2 tbsp baking soda
- 1/2 tbsp baking powder
- 1-1/2 tbsp vanilla
- 2-1/2 cups flour
- 2 apples, finely diced.

Streusel
- 1 stick butter
- 1/2 cup brown sugar
- 1/2 cup flour
- 1/2 cup oats
- 1/2 tbsp cinnamon

Glaze
- 2 cups powdered sugar
- 1 tbsp apple cinnamon blend
- 3 tbsp milk

1. Preheat your Grill to 325^{0}F.
2. Add the cake ingredients except for the apples in a blender and pulse until well-combined .fold in the diced apples.
3. Spread the mixture on a 9x13 baking pan.
4. Mix the streusel ingredients using hands until crumbly then pour the mixture over the cake mixture.
5. Place the baking pan at the top rack of your Grill to create a space between the cake pan and the fire.
6. Bake for 45 minutes or until the tester comes out with moist crumbs only.
7. Let rest for 10 minutes before serving.

Grilled Beef Pot Pie

Prep time: 25 minutes, Cook time: 60 minutes; Serves 8

Ingredients

- 1 pie crust

Pot Pie
- 2 cups potatoes, diced
- 3 cups leftover pot roast
- 1 cup corn
- 1 cup carrots
- 1/2 cup peas
- 1/2 cup green beans

Gravy
- 1/4 cup butter +2 tbsp
- 1/4 cup flour
- 3 cups beef broth
- 1/4 tbsp sherry
- 1/2 tbsp onion powder
- 1/8 tbsp garlic powder
- 1/4 thyme

Egg Wash
- 1 egg yolk
- 1 tbsp water

1. Preheat your Grill to 350^{0}F.

2. Take the potatoes and drizzle with some oil then sprinkle with salt. Microwave them for 4 minutes.
3. Place the pot pie ingredients in a cast iron pan.
4. Melt butter in a nonstick skillet, then whisk in flour until there are no lumps.
5. Stir cook the mixture for 7 minutes over medium heat. Whisk in broth, sherry, onion powder, garlic powder, and thyme.
6. Pour the mixture over the meat and vegetables. Top everything with a pie crust and slits for vents.
7. Whisk together the egg wash ingredients and brush the mixture at the top of the bowl.
8. Place the pie in the Grill, close the lid, and cook for 1 hour or until the internal temperature reaches 165^0F. Cover the pie with a foil if it gets too much dark.
9. Let rest for 10 minutes before serving.

Grilled Apple Crisp

Prep time: 20 minutes, Cook time: 1 hour; Serves 15

Ingredients

Apple
- 10 apples, washed, peeled and cored
- 1/2 cup four
- 1 cup dark brown sugar
- 1/2 tbsp cinnamon
- 1/2 cup butter

Crisp
- 3 cups oatmeal, old fashioned
- 1-1/2 cups flour
- 1-1/2 cups salted butter
- 1-1/2 tbsp cinnamon
- Cups brown sugar

Preparation Method

1. Preheat your Grill to 350^0F.

2. Slice the apples into cubes then toss with flour, sugar, and cinnamon
3. Spray cooking spray on a 10x12 foil grill pan, then place the apples in it.place the butter randomly on the apples.
4. In a mixing bowl, mix the crisp ingredients until well combined. Place the mixture over the apples.
5. Place the grill pan at the hottest part of the Grill and cook while checking every 20 minutes.
6. Remove the pan from the Grill when the edges are bubbly, the topping is golden brown and the apples are tender.
7. Let rest for 25 minutes before serving.

Berry Cobbler

Prep time: 15 minutes, Cook time: 35 minutes; Serves 8

Ingredients

Fruit Filling
- 3 cups berries, mixed(blueberries, blackberries, raspberries)
- 1 cup brown sugar
- 1 lemon juice
- 1 tbsp lemon zest
- 1 tbsp vanilla extract
- 1 pinch salt

Cobbler Topping
- 1-1/2 cups flour, all-purpose
- 3 tbsp granulated sugar
- 1-1/2 tbsp baking powder
- 1/2 tbsp salt
- 8 tbsp cold butter
- 1/2 cup sour cream
- 2 tbsp sugar

Preparation Method

1. Fire up the Grill to smoke setting for 5 minutes with the lid open or until the fire has been established, then preheat it to

350^{0}F with the lid closed

2. Combine berries, sugar, juice, zest, vanilla, and salt in a mixing bowl until the fruits are well coated.
3. Place the fruit mixture in an 8x8 aluminum pan. Make cobbler topping by mixing all-purpose flour, brown sugar, baking powder, and salt in a mixing bowl. Cut the butter in the flour into pea-size pieces.
4. Stir in sour cream until the dough starts to come together. Pinch the dough into small pieces placing them on top of the fruits until well covered.
5. Top with sugar if you desire.
6. Put the grill pan on the grill grate and cook for 35 minutes or until the top is golden brown.
7. Carefully remove the pan from the Grill and let rest for a few minutes to Serve.

Smoked Mac and Cheese

Prep time: 2 minutes, Cook time: 1 hour; Serves 8

Ingredients

- 1/2 cup salted butter
- 1/3 cup flour
- 6 cups whole milk
- 1/2 tbsp salt
- 1/2 tbsp dry mustard
- A dash of Worcestershire
- White sauce
- noodles
- 1 lb small shells, cooked in saltwater
- 2 cups cheddar jack cheese
- 2 cups white cheddar, smoked
- 1 cup ritz, crushed

Preparation Method

1. Startup the Grill and set it to smoke with the lid open. Let it run for 10 minutes then turn the grill up to 325^{0}F with the lid

closed.

2. Meanwhile, melt butter in a saucepan over medium heat. Whisk in flour, reduce heat and continue whisking for 6 minutes or until it turns into light tan color.
3. Stir in milk, salt, dry mustard, and Worcestershire. increase the heat to medium and cook while stirring until the sauce has thickened.
4. Stir in white sauce, noodles, small shells, and all cheeses in 1 cup in a baking dish sprayed with cooking spray.
5. Top with ritz and the remaining cheese. Place the baking dish in the Grill and bake for 30 minutes.

Banana Foster

Prep Time: 10 minutes/ Cook Time 15-20 minutes / Serves: 4

Ingredients:

- 10 bananas, overripe, peeled and halved lengthwise
- Rum and raisin sauce for serving

Directions:

1. Pre-heat your Grill to 250 degrees F
2. Take a large-sized disposable aluminum foil, arrange bananas in a single layer
3. Transfer to Grill and smoke for 15-20 minutes
4. Serve with rum and raisin sauce, enjoy!

Dump Cake

Prep Time: 10 minutes/ Cook Time 30-45 minutes / Serves: 4

Ingredients:

- 1 box cake mix of your choosing
- 2 cans of your desired pie filling
- 1 stick of butter

Directions:

1. Pre-heat your Grill to 375 degrees F and set it indirect cooking
2. Spread the contents of the pie to the bottom of a pan, sprinkle cake mix on top
3. Melt butter in a saucepot and drizzle over cake mix
4. Transfer to the Grill and bake for about 45 minutes
5. Enjoy!

Healthy Cheese Cake

Prep Time: 10 minutes/ Cook Time 10 minutes / Serves: 4

Ingredients:

- 4 tablespoons unsalted butter
- 6 tablespoons all-purpose flour
- 1 cup milk
- 1 beer
- 2 teaspoons Dijon mustard
- 1 teaspoon garlic powder
- 1 teaspoon salt
- 1 teaspoon cayenne pepper
- 6 cups sharp cheddar cheese

Directions:

1. Pre-heat your Grill to 400 degrees F
2. Take a large steel bowl and melt in butter, whisk in flour and mix well to make a roux
3. Place it overheat and slowly keep heating it until milky smooth
4. Add remaining ingredients to the bowl and transfer to Grill, cook for about 10 minutes until the cheese is completely smooth
5. Serve and enjoy!

Herby Cheese Crackers

Prep Time: 10 minutes/ Cook Time 15 minutes / Serves: 4

Ingredients:

- 1/3 cup olive oil
- 1 pack of ranch dressing mix
- 1 tablespoon dried dill
- 1 tablespoon garlic powder
- 1 tablespoon mix of dill and citrus
- 12 ounces box of Cheez-It Snack Crackers, Baked, Original
- 11-ounce box of Nabisco Saltine Crackers, Premium, Mini

Directions:

1. Pre-heat your Grill to 250 degrees F
2. Take a bowl and whisk in first four ingredients, divide in half
3. Drizzle half of the liquid over the cheese crackers in a large-sized bowl
4. Spread the mixture over a round cooking grid and transfer to Grill, bake for 15 minutes, making sure to keep stirring it after every 5 minutes
5. Let it cool and repeat the mixture with saltines
6. Once they are cooled, toss both together and serve
7. Enjoy!

Brie Cheese Dish

Prep Time: 10 minutes/ Cook Time 60 minutes / Serves: 4

Ingredients:

- 8-ounce blocks of brie cheese

Directions:

1. Pre-heat your Grill to 90 degrees Flow settings
2. Add cheese blocks to your Grill and let them smoke for 4 hours

3. Remove from heat and let them cool at room temperature
4. Transfer to a container, serve, and enjoy!

Queso Chorizo

Prep Time: 10 minutes/ Cook Time 60 minutes / Serves: 4

Ingredients:

- ounces cubed Velveeta cheese
- 4 ounces cream cheese, cubed
- 10 ounces Rotel
- 1 pound cooked Chorizo, chopped

Directions:

1. Pre-heat your Grill to 200 degrees F
2. Add all of the ingredients in an aluminum foil pan and smoke for 1 hour, stirring after every 15 minutes
3. Serve with tortilla chips
4. Enjoy!

Peach Parfait

Prep Time: 10 minutes/ Cook Time 30-50 minutes / Serves: 4

Ingredients:

- 4 barely ripe peaches, halved and pitted
- 1 tablespoon of firmly packed brown sugar
- 1 pint of vanilla ice cream
- 3 tablespoon of honey

Directions:

1. Pre-heat your Grill to 200 degrees Fahrenheit
2. Sprinkle cut peach halves with brown sugar
3. Transfer them to Grill and smoke for 33-45 minutes
4. Transfer the peach halves to dessert plates and top with vanilla ice cream
5. Drizzle honey and serve!

Fine Grilled Pumpkin Squash

Prep Time: 10 minutes/ Cook Time 60 minutes / Serves: 4

Ingredients:

- 4 pumpkin squash, halved horizontally with the pulp and seeds discarded
- 3 tablespoon of olive oil
- Salt as needed
- Freshly ground black pepper
- 8 ounce of dry seasoned stuffing mix
- 1/2 a cup of hot water
- 1/2 a cup of melted butter
- 1 eaten egg
- 1/2 a cup of chopped celery
- 1/2 a cup of chopped onion
- 2 teaspoon of chili powder
- Spicy mustard for drizzle

Directions:

1. Pre-heat your Grill to 225 degrees Fahrenheit
2. Lightly drizzle the squash halves with olive oil and sprinkle pepper and salt
3. Take a medium bowl and stir in stuffing mix, butter, water, egg, onion, celery, chili powder
4. Stuff the mix into the squash halves and transfer the squash to the Grill rack
5. Smoke for 1 and a 1/2 hours
6. Drizzle with spicy mustard and enjoy!

Unique Baba Ganoush

Prep Time: 10 minutes/ Cook Time 60-90 minutes /
Serves: 4

Ingredients:

- 1 eggplant halved lengthwise
- 1 tablespoon of olive oil
- 2 and a 1/2 teaspoon of salt

- 2 and a 1/2 tablespoon of tahini
- Juice of 1 lemon
- 1 garlic clove minced
- 2 tablespoon of chopped fresh parsley
- Pita chips

Directions:

1. Pre-heat your Grill to 200 degrees Fahrenheit
2. Rub eggplant halves with olive oil and sprinkle 2 teaspoons of salt
3. Place the halves o Grill rack and Grill for about 1 and a 1/2 hours
4. Remove and peel off the skin, discard it
5. Transfer eggplant flesh to a food processor
6. Add tahini, garlic, lemon juice, 1/ a teaspoon of salt and blend well
7. Transfer to a storage
8. Stir in parsley and serve with pita chips
9. Enjoy!

Chapter 7: Grilling and Roasting Recipes

Mushroom with Fennel Dressed with Roasted Chicken

Prep time and Cooking Time: 22 hours 50 minutes | Serves: 4

Ingredients To Use:

- 8 sun-dried tomatoes, oil-packed
- 4pound chicken
- Salt with black pepper
- 1-1/2 Tbsp of thyme
- 10 ounces of mushroom, preferably white button
- 1/2 pound of crusty bread
- 4 cloves of garlic, preferably smashed
- 1 Tbsp of balsamic vinegar
- 2 Tbsp of butter without salt.
- 1 fennel bulb

Step-by-Step Directions::

1. Rub black pepper and salt all over the chicken, including cavities. Keep in the refrigerator for 22 hours.
2. Remove chicken from the refrigerator and rub with butter. In a big bowl, mix sun-dried tomato, mushroom, fennel, garlic, thyme, salt, and pepper. Then put the mixture into the roasting pan along with the chicken.
3. Roast the chicken on the preheated grill for 35 minutes. Flip the chicken with a tong and roast for another 15 minutes, or until the internal temperature of the thigh reads between 165-170^{0}F.

Roasted Steak

Prep time and Cooking Time: 12 hours 30 minutes | Serves: 5

Ingredients To Use:

- 2 Tbsp of rosemary, preferably freshly chopped
- 2 tsp of salt
- 1 Tbsp of thyme, preferably fresh leaves
- 1/2 cup of olive oil
- 1-1/2 tsp of black pepper
- 1 of 3-inch steak
- 5 cloves of garlic, preferably thinly sliced

Step-to-step Direction to Cook It:

1. Make the marinade by cooking garlic until it is soft, then add rosemary and thyme. Cook for about 1 minute.
2. Rub black pepper and salt all over the steak, then put it inside a Ziploc bag with the garlic mixture. Keep in the refrigerator overnight.
3. Remove steak from the refrigerator the next morning, and discard the garlic marinade. Roast the steak on the preheated grill for 30 minutes or until the internal temperature reads 160°F.
4. Serve the steak and season with salt and black pepper before eating.

Sweet Potato Spiced Fries

Prep time and Cooking Time: 30 minutes | Serves: 4

Ingredients To Use:

- 1 tsp of kosher salt
- 2 Tbsp of olive oil
- 1 tsp of paprika
- 1/2 tsp of cumin, ground
- 2 pounds of sliced sweet potatoes
- 1 tsp of brown sugar, light
- 1 tsp of chili powder
- 1 tsp of garlic powder

Step-by-Step Directions:

1. Mix the brown sugar, paprika, garlic powder, chili powder, salt, and cumin in a bowl.
2. Mix the sliced potatoes and oil in a separate bowl, then add the brown sugar mixture and toss well. Pour the coated potatoes into a roasting pan and roast until it is brown and tender. This will take about 15-20 minutes.
3. Serve as soon as possible.

Sweet Marinated Grilled Spare Ribs

Prep time: 15 minutes| Cook time: 2hours 30 minutes| Serves: 5

Ingredients:

- 5 racks of spare ribs, membrane removed.

Marinade

- 2 medium red onions, chopped
- 2 Tbsp honey
- 1 Tbsp sugar
- 4 Tbsp soy sauce
- 2 tbsp rice wine vinegar
- 1 Tsp sea salt
- 4 garlic cloves, minced
- 1/4 cup thyme leaves
- Cayenne pepper (sprinkle)

Directions:

1. Preheat Grill for indirect cooking with

Iron Cast Grid to 302^{0}F

2. Prepare marinade by adding onion, honey, soy sauce, vinegar, garlic, and salt to a food processor. Process ingredients until smooth.
3. Marinate the spare ribs, and then arrange the marinated ribs on the roasting rack.
4. Place the rack containing spare ribs on the grill. Close the lid of the Grill and allow ribs to cook for 2 hours.
5. Open the Grill lid and apply a generous amount of marinade on the spare ribs, leave to cook for another 30 minutes.
6. Remove the flank steak from the grid and arrange it on a platter. Slice the steak, sprinkle with cayenne pepper and serve the grilled steak.

Grilled Blade Steak

Prep time: 10 minutes| Cook time: 10 minutes| Serves: 4

Ingredients:

- 4 slices of blade steak, fat layer removed
- Ground pepper(optional)
- Salt(optional)
- Fresh coriander, chopped(optional)
- Red cherry tomatoes, chopped(optional)

Directions:

1. Preheat the Grill to 482^{0}F.
2. Place the steaks on the grid in the Grill and grill for 6 minutes. Give the steak a quarter turn after 3 minutes to create a grill pattern.
3. Take out the steaks and leave on a platter to rest for some minutes. Serve with pepper, salt, fresh coriander, and tomatoes.

Asian Marinated Steaks

Prep time: 24 hours 5 minutes| Cook time: 18 minutes| Serves: 4

Ingredients:

- 1/2 cup fresh scallions, sliced
- 1/2 cup fresh pineapple juice
- 1/4 roughly chopped ginger
- 2lb flank steak
- 1/2 cup canola oil
- 1 Tbsp five-spice powder
- 10 garlic cloves, chopped
- 1Tbsp chili garlic sauce

Directions:

1. Whisk together pineapple juice, canola oil, scallions, ginger, garlic, chili garlic sauce, soy sauce, and five-spice powder.
2. Put the steak into a large Ziploc bag, pour marinade into the bag, then seal it.
3. Place the Ziploc in a refrigerator and leave for a whole day, flip the bag over at intervals.
4. Separate steak from marinade and get rid of the marinade.
5. Put the steak on the grid in the Grill and close the lid. Grill steak for 8 minutes, then turn the side over after 4 minutes.
6. Remove flank steak from the grid and place steak on a platter. Leave to rest for 5 minutes, and then carve to desired slices.

Livar Pork Neck with Apricots

Prep time: 15 minutes| Cook time: 1 hour | Serves: 6

Ingredients:

- 3 lb livar pork neck, cut horizontally to 1-1/2 cm thick
- 10 soft apricots, dried and cut into strips
- A handful of sage, cut into strips
- 3 Tbsp hot coarse mustard
- 1 Tsp ground pepper

- Salt
- A handful of lemon thyme

Directions:

1. Preheat the Grill with the Cast Iron Grid to 302°F
2. Add pepper and salt to the pork neck, and then rub mustard over it. Spread stripped sage and apricot across the meat, fold the meat up and hold it in place with butcher's string.
3. Slip lemon thyme in between roast and string. Transfer the roast to the grid and grill. Flip roast every 10 minutes and grill to complete doneness with an internal temperature of 154°F.
4. Take out the roast and place it on an aluminum foil for 30 minutes to continue cooking.
5. Cut the roast into the desired size and serve.

Lamb Cutlets with Mint Chimichurri

Prep time: 5 minutes| Cook time: 5 minutes| Serves: 6

Ingredients:

- 12 lamb cutlets(about 4 ounces)
- 1/2 cup lemon juice
- Olive oil
- Kosher salt
- Freshly ground pepper
- 1/2 bunch fresh oregano, chopped
- Chimichurri Sauce
- 2 garlic cloves, minced
- 1 red bell pepper, seeded and chopped
- 1 large red onion, chopped
- 3-1/2 Tbsp red wine vinegar
- 1/2 cup of olive oil
- 3 Tbs capers

Directions:

1. Place a small saucepan on the cooking grid over medium-low heat. Stir in salt and water, then cook until salt dissolves. Pour salted water in a bowl and leave to cool. Mix garlic, oil, vinegar, onion, caper, salted water, and vinegar in a small bowl.
2. In another small bowl, whisk together lemon juice, oregano, pepper, and salt. Brush the oregano mixture over the cutlets and leave to rest for 30 minutes.
3. Oil the cutlet with a brush and arrange cutlets on the Cast Iron Grid. Cover the lid of the Grill and allow cutlets to cook on both sides for 6 minutes
4. Remove cutlets and place on a platter.
5. Serve with Chimichurri sauce.

T-Bone Steaks

Prep time: 5 minutes| Cook time: 10 minutes| Serves: 4

Ingredients:

- 4 T-bone steaks, roughly about 3lbs (above 2.5cm thick)

Directions:

1. Add a dash of salt to each steak and arrange steaks on the grid with ends facing 10 and 4 o'clock. Close the lid of and grill. After about 2 minutes, flip the steak clockwise with ends facing 2 and 8 o'clock to create a diamond pattern.
2. Turn the steak over and repeat the actions above until the desired degree of doneness is reached, and a diamond grill pattern is gotten. Cover the lid of Grill after each step.
3. Remove steak from the grid, allow to rest for some minutes, and then cut into desired slices.

Maple Glazed Grilled Salmon

Prep time: 25 hours 6 minutes| Cook time: 15 minutes| Serves: 5

Ingredients:

- 5 oz skinless salmon fillet
- 1 Tsp kosher salt
- 2 Tbsp canola oil
- 1 tbsp cayenne pepper

Marinade

- 1/4 cup lemon juice
- 1 cup maple syrup
- 1/4 cup cooked horseradish, tightly packed

Directions:

1. Prepare the marinade by adding ingredients in a bowl, and then whisk to combine.
2. Put salmon into a large Ziploc bag. Pour marinade into the bag and then seal bag.
3. Place the Ziploc bag in a refrigerator and leave for a whole day. Flip the bag over at intervals.
4. Soak cedar plank in water for 60 minutes.
5. Take out the plank from water and place the plank directly on the grid.
6. Heat the plank for 6 minutes with closed Grill lid. Turn over the plank in between.
7. Apply canola oil on the plank with a brush.
8. Separate salmon from marinade and get rid of the marinade.
9. Set salmon fillets on the plank and sprinkle pepper and salt over it.
10. Close the lid of and grill salmon for 15 minutes, until fish flakes

CÔTE DE BOEUF/Beef Ribs

Prep time: 15 minutes| Cook time: 1hour5 minutes| Serves: 2

Ingredients:

- 2 côtes de boeuf (about 6cm thick)

- 2 cloves garlic, minced (optional)
- 2 sprigs rosemary (optional)

Directions:

1. Salt the côtes de boeuf and arrange them on the grid. Close the lid of the Grill and cook for 60 minutes until an internal temperature of 125.6^{0}F is obtained, which can be measured with the Instant Read Digital Thermometer.
2. Take out the cotes from the grid and place aluminum foil over it.
3. Using the Grit Lifter, replace the grid and Plate Setter with the Cast Iron Grid.
4. Pre heat Grill to 482^{0}F. Arrange the cotes on the grid and grill for about 2 minutes. Give the cotes a quarter turn every minute to produce grill patterns and continue grilling till a core temperature of 131^{0}F is obtained
5. Place grilled meat on a platter and cut meat after 10 minutes.

Grilled Top Sirloin Steak

Prep time: 15 minutes| Cook time: 1hour5 minutes| Serves: 2

Ingredients:

- 2 lb top sirloin steak with fat cap
- Kosher salt
- Ground black pepper

Directions:

1. Preheat Grill to 350^{0}F with the Roasting and Drip Pan under the Iron Cast Grid.
2. Place meat on a flat workspace and split the fatty surface of the meat with a sharp knife.
3. Season the meat with salt and pepper as desired, then leave to rest for 5 minutes.
4. Insert the Insert Read Digital thermometer into the meat and transfer the beef to the preheated grid with the

fatty surface up.

5. Cover the lid of the Grill and cook steak for 50minutes, until the internal core temperature is 135F for medium-rare.
6. Take out the meat from Grill and place it on an aluminum foil.
7. Take out the Iron Cast grid, Roasting and Drip Pan, and Plate Setter with the aid of a grill gripper.
8. Replace the cast grid in the Grill. Cook the meat on the grid again for a few minutes with the fatty side down.
9. Remove meat and place on a platter for 10 minutes.
10. Cut into slices and serve.

Grilled Beef Roll Stuffed with Marinated Spring Onions

Prep time: 10 minutes| Cook time: 6 minutes| Serves: 4

Ingredients:

- 8 slices entrecote of approximately 1lb, (each slice about 3mm)
- 4 Tbsp sesame oil
- 4 Tbsp Ketjab manis
- 8 spring onions, cut into rings
- 4 Tbsp mirin
- 4 Tbsp sweet chili sauce
- 2 cloves garlic, finely chopped

Directions:

1. Preheat Grill with Cast Iron Grid to 428^{0}F
2. Whisk together mirin, sesame oil, garlic, Ketjab, chili sauce, and garlic in a bowl. Add onions into the marinade.
3. Lay entrecote slices on a flat surface and then spread marinate at the bottom of the entrecote. Roll up the entrecote and use a cocktail stick to put it in place.
4. Arrange rolled up slices on the grid in the Grill. Grill for 6 minutes, flipping beef

rolls over once and cover the lid of the Grill.

5. Take out rolls from the grid and serve.

Grilled Asparagus

Prep time: 5 minutes| Cook time: 10 minutes| Serves: 3

Ingredients:

- 12 fresh white asparagus, peeled and trimmed
- 3 hard-boiled eggs, chopped
- Sunflower oil

Directions:

1. Preheat the Grill to 320^{0}F.
2. Brush sunflower oil over the asparagus.
3. Arrange the asparagus in parallel directions on the grid.
4. Cook for 10 minutes. Press down the asparagus and use an iron spatula to turn the asparagus after 6 minutes. Close the Grill lid and allow asparagus to cook until fork tender.
5. Take out asparagus from the grid and serve with chopped eggs.

Brine and Roasted Turkey

Prep time: 13 hours | Cook time: 1 hour 20 minutes | Serves: 8

Ingredients:

- 16 ounces of defrosted turkey
- 2-1/2 cups kosher salt
- 2 gallons of water
- 2-1/2 cups brown sugar
- 2-1/2 Tbsp dill and herbs seasoning
- 1 bunch thyme
- 1 bunch rosemary
- 1 cup white wine
- 1 bunch sage
- 2 carrots
- 2 celery stalk, sliced

- 1 lemon, sliced
- 1 yellow onion, sliced
- 3 sticks unsalted butter

Directions:

1. Add the salt, brown sugar, seasoning, and water to a pot. Bring the mixture (brine) to a boil, then chill.
2. Submerge the turkey in the brine and refrigerate for 13 hours (preferably overnight). Remove turkey, rinse, and pat dry with a paper towel. Allow the turkey to rest for 1 hour at room temperature.
3. Adjust the Grill to a temperature of 325^{0}F
4. Place the turkey in the Grill roasting rack, melt two sticks of butter, and add 1 Tbsp of thyme, sage, and rosemary. Melt the remaining stick of butter, brush the skin of the turkey. Pour the butter mixture over the turkey, ensure there is total coverage. Add a drip pan to catch the drippings.
5. Stuff the turkey with onion, celery, carrots, sage, thyme, and rosemary. Pour the cup of white wine in the drip pan.
6. Fill a Ziploc bag with ice and place on the turkey breast for 30 minutes to reduce the temperature. Cook the turkey on the Grill until the internal temperature measures 165^{0}F

Roasted lamb leg

Prep time: 10 minutes | Cook time: 7 hours 25minutes | Serves: 6

Ingredients:

- 6 lb lamb leg
- 1 tsp kosher salt
- 20 pieces of fresh rosemary, 1-inch each
- 1 tsp of freshly grounded black pepper

- 5 cloves garlic, thinly sliced
- 1/4 cup extra-virgin olive oil

Directions:

1. Preheat the Grill to 300°F
2. On the lamb, make 20 (1-inch) cuts all over it, stuff the hole with rosemary and garlic. Brush the olive oil on the lamb and season with pepper and salt
3. Place the lamb on a rack and position the drip pan, then close the Grill.
4. Roast for 2 hours or until internal temperature reads 140°F. Remove from heat and allow to cool for 10 minutes.
5. Cut and serve.

Plank Roasted Pears

Prep time: 20 minutes | Cook time: 20 minutes | Serves: 6

Ingredients:

- 4 large ripe pears
- 2 Tbsp of melted unsalted butter
- 1/2 cup of blue cheese, crumbled
- 2 Tbsp amber honey
- 2 cedar grilling planks, soaked in water for 1 hour

Directions:

1. Set Grill at 350°F for direct cooking.
2. Halve the pear lengthwise and remove apple cores. Cut the halved pear side up.
3. Mix wildflower honey and melted butter in a bowl, use the mixt to brush the open surface of the pear and sprinkle with crumbled cheese.
4. Arrange soaked planks over the cooking grid and cover Grill for 3-5 minutes or until the planks begin to smoke. Open Grill, use a grill gripper to turn over the plank, then swiftly put the pear on the grid with the open side up.
5. Roast for 12-15 minutes.

Roasted Nashville Cauliflower wings

Prep time: 15 minutes | Cook time: 30 minutes | Serves: 4

Ingredients:

- 1 head of cauliflower florets
- 2 Tbsp Nashville hot seasoning
- 1/2 Tbsp minced garlic
- Extra virgin olive oil
- 1 cup melted butter

Directions:

1. Preheat the Grill to 400°F
2. Mix cauliflower with olive oil and place on the cooking grid. Roast the cauliflower for 25 minutes or until tender and slightly brown.
3. Mix the butter, Nashville hot seasoning, and garlic in a bowl.
4. Remove cauliflower from the Grill and transfer to a large bowl; pour your seasoning mixture on the cauliflower and mix.
5. Serve immediately.

Roasted Halibut with Greek Relish

Prep time: 1 hour | Cook time: 20 minutes | Serves: 6

Ingredients:

- 2 lb. fresh Halibut fillet
- 2 cans of Red gold tomatoes (diced and drained)
- 3 oz. dry feta cheese
- 10 0z. Kalamata olives (sliced 1/4 inch
- 1/4 cup extra virgin olive oil
- 1 onion (diced)
- 3 cloves of garlic (minced)
- 10 fresh basil

- 1/2 Tbsp kosher salt
- 2 Tbsp red wine vinegar
- 2 Tbsp of salad oil
- 1/2 Tbsp black pepper (ground)

Directions:

1. To make the relish, add all the ingredients (except the fillet) to a blender and t process until smooth. Refrigerate mixture for a 30 minutes-2hours
2. Install Plate Setter for indirect cooking at 400^0F
3. Season the fillet lightly with salt and black pepper, place on the Grill and roast for 8-10 minutes or until fish begins to flake.
4. Place a small amount of the relish on the fish and allow it to warm through.
5. Remove the fish from heat and place on a small pile of relish; allow the heat of the fish to warm the relish.
6. Serve warm.

Roasted Chicken with lemon, Garlic, and Rosemary

Prep time: 15 minutes | Cook time: 1 hour 45 minutes | Serves: 4

Ingredients:

- 4lb chicken
- 1 lemon, halved
- 3 cloves of garlic, halved
- 3 sprigs of rosemary
- 1 Tbsp extra virgin olive oil
- 1 Tbsp kosher salt
- 1 tsp ground black pepper

Directions:

1. Set the Grill for indirect cooking at 400^0F
2. Rinse the chicken with cold water and pat dry. Sprinkle the chicken with salt and pepper.
3. Pluck the leaves from one sprig of rosemary and sprinkle on the chicken, place the other two sprigs of rosemary along with the garlic and lemon inside the cavity
4. Place the chicken on the Grill and roast the chicken for 1 hour or until the skin is brown and crispy. Continue to roast until the internal temperature is 165^0F
5. Remove and allow to sit for 5 minutes, and serve

Roasted Broccoli Salad

Prep time: 15minutes | Cook time: 40minutes | Serves: 2

Ingredients:

- 1 head of broccoli (broken into bits)
- 3 Tbsp olive oil
- 1 Tbsp minced garlic
- 1-1/2 tsp salt
- 1/2 yellow onion (diced)
- 1/2 tsp ground black pepper
- 1 Tbsp red wine vinegar
- 1 cup mayonnaise
- 1 cup blue cheese crumble
- 1 cup crumbled bacon
- 1 tsp pepper

Directions:

1. Set the Grill for indirect cooking at 400^0F
2. In a bowl, add the olive oil, broccoli, salt, and pepper. Mix thoroughly. Place the broccoli in the Grill iron skillet and roast for 25 minutes or until tender.
3. In a bowl, add mayonnaise, red wine vinegar, blue cheese, ground black pepper, and salt mix well together to make your dressing
4. Remove the roasted broccoli from the skillet and allow it to cool. Place bacon

on the skillet and cook for 5 minutes or until slightly crispy, add onions and cook for another 3 minutes. Remove the skillet, add garlic, and stir the mix.

5. Mix the bacon and broccoli, stir in your dressing and allow the mixture to cool for 4 hours.

Roasted Corn and Green Chili Cheese Spread

Prep time: 10 minutes | Cook time: 20 minutes | Serves: 4

Ingredients:

- 2 medium ears of corn
- 1 cup mayonnaise
- 2 cups shredded cheddar cheese
- 2 Tbsp of reduced-sodium roasted chicken base
- 1/2 tsp pepper
- 2 Tbsp hot sauce
- 1 can of diced chili pepper, rinsed and drained

Directions:

1. Preheat the Grill to 400°F
2. Wrap ears of the corn in foil and cook for 20 minutes or until tender. Remove the corns from the cob.
3. In a large bowl, combine mayonnaise, reduced-sodium base, original hot sauce, and black pepper. Mix thoroughly. Add cheddar cheese, roasted corn kernels, and green chiles. Blend well.
4. Refrigerate and serve.

Smoke-Roasted Oyster and Clams

Prep time: 20 minutes | Cook time: 10 minutes | Serves: 4

Ingredients:

- 16 fresh oyster, top shell removed
- 16 fresh clams
- 1 bunch sliced scallions
- 2 jalapenos, seeded and minced
- 1 cup of wine
- 8 strip bacon, cut into 1/4 inch slivers
- 1/4 cups of minced parsley
- Hot sauce
- 4 Tbsp unsalted butter

Directions:

1. In Dutch Oven, melt 1 Tbsp butter; add scallions, jalapenos, and beacons. Cook until the bacon is golden brown. Stir in the dill.
2. Set Grill for direct cooking at 500°F with wood chunks or chips
3. Loosen the oyster from the bottom shell; try not to spill the juice. Carefully arrange the oyster on a wire rack, then place a spoonful of the bacon mixture in each shell. Remember to save some for the clams.
4. Arrange the clams in a grill basket. Reheat the leftover beacon mixture, add the white wine and cook until the wine is reduced. Whisk in the remaining butter.
5. Place the oyster on a wire rack in the grill grate and roast for 5 minutes or until the bacon begins to sizzle. Remove oysters from the grate and replace it with the clam in the grill basket. Cook for 4 minutes or until clam begins to open. Discard any clam that fails to open. Place the clam in the wine and bacon mixture and stir
6. Serve with hot sauce

Grilled Mahi-Mahi with Roasted Yellow Pepper Coulis

Prep time: 1 hour | Cook time: 20 minutes | Serves: 4

Ingredients:

- 4 fillets of Mahi-Mahi (6oz. each)
- 2 yellow peppers
- 1 tsp lemon juice
- 1/4 cup of heavy cream
- 1 Tbsp extra virgin olive oil
- 1/4 cup olive oil
- 1/2 tsp sugar
- Salt and pepper to taste

Directions:

1. Season the fillets with salt, pepper, and 1 Tbsp olive oil. Marinate for 1 hour
2. Set the Grill for direct cooking at 500°F
3. Brush the yellow pepper with olive oil and roast on the cooking grid, turning regularly for 5 minutes or until soft. Remove and place in a sealed container for 5 minutes. When the peppers are cool enough, remove the seed, skin, and stem. In a food processor, add the pepper, lemon juice, sugar, salt, cream, and olive oil. Puree until smooth, remove in a small pot and keep warm.
4. Grill the fish 3minutes for each side. Serve with the sauce.

Honey-Roasted Black Pepper Corn

Prep time: 15 minutes| Cook time: 20 minutes | Serves: 4

Ingredients:

- 4 corn on the cob, husk intact
- 1 Tbsp seasoned vegetable base
- 1 Tbsp honey
- 1/4 cup melted butter
- 1/2 tsp black pepper

Directions:

1. Set Grill for direct cooking at 400°F
2. Soak corn with the husk intact in cold water
3. In a bowl, mix the honey, vegetable base, black pepper, and butter. Remove the corn from water, pull the husk but don't remove, remove the corn hairs. Brush the mixture on the corn and when it is well coated, pull the husk over the corn
4. Using a tongue, place the corn onto the Grill, turn every 3 minutes. Cook the corn for 15-20 minutes or until it is soft to touch.

Chapter 8: Smoking Recipes

Smoked Porchetta

Prep time: 24 hours | Cook time: 6 hours | Serves: 4

Ingredients:

- 4 lb. pork belly
- 4-star anise, ground
- 1 cup kosher salt
- 5 allspices, ground
- 10 black peppercorn, ground
- 10 white peppercorn, ground
- 3 sprigs thyme, chopped
- 10 garlic cloves, smashed
- 1/2 cup granulated sugar

Directions:

1. Mix all the ingredients and apply them to the pork belly on both sides. This should be done 24 hours before you cook. Cure the pork belly in a cooler
2. Set Grill for indirect cooking with Plate Setter at 250^{0}F
3. Rinse off the cure, tie the pork belly into a roll with butchers twine. Place the meat in the Grill and smoke for 4-6 hours until the pork is tender or reach an internal temperature of 165^{0}F.
4. Remove from Grill, untie and allow to rest for 10 minutes.

Smoked Beef Rib with Mustard Marinade

Prep time: 30 minutes | Cook time: 6 hours | Serves: 7

Ingredients:

- 1 cup honey
- 1/2 cup vinegar
- 1/2 cup mustard
- 1 cup apple cider
- 2 Tbsp ancho powder
- 1/4 cup grounded garlic
- 1/4 cup black pepper
- 3/4 cup of brown sugar
- 1 tsp ground cayenne
- 1 cup of kosher salt
- 1/2 cup bouillon paste
- 2 Tbsp ground lemon pepper
- 1/2 cup of Worcestershire sauce
- 6 pounds beef ribs, block cut
- 1 cup beer, brown ale

Directions:

1. Set the Grill for indirect cooking with Plate Setter at 250^{0}F
2. To make the mustard marinade, add the Worcestershire sauce, vinegar, yellow mustard, mustard, and water in a bowl. Mix well together. Set aside. To prepare the seasoning, add the kosher salt, black pepper, powder, lemon pepper, ancho powder, and cayenne pepper in a bowl. Mix the seasoning ingredients thoroughly together
3. Brush the beef with the mustard mixture and season on both sides. Place the seasoned meat in the Grill and smoke for 5 hours. While smoking, add the honey, brown sugar, bouillon paste, and beer to a bowl. Mix your honey-beer glaze thoroughly.
4. Remove the beef from Grill and slather with the glaze, wrap with aluminum foil and place back on the Grill. Smoke for 1hr

Smoked Spicy Korean Rib

Prep time: 20 minutes | Cook time: 5 hours | Serves: 4

Ingredients:

- 2 racks of pork ribs, with removed membranes
- 1/4 cup beer
- 1/4 cup of butter
- Salt and pepper
- Korean Barbeque sauce (recipe in chapter 9)

Directions:

1. Install Plate Setter for indirect cooking at 275°F. Use hickory wood and position drip pan containing water below the grill.
2. Mix salt and pepper to form a rub, then coat the ribs with the rub. Put the coated ribs on the grid and cook for 3 hours.
3. Move the ribs and place with side facing down on foil paper. Add beer and butter. Cover the ribs with another foil paper and continue cooking for 1 hour
4. Discard the foil papers and raise the temperature of the Grill to 300°F. Glaze the rib with Korean barbeque sauce and cook for another 1 hour or until tender.
5. Remove and serve.

Smoked Chicken Ravioli

Prep time: 30 minutes|Cook time: 2 hours 30 minutes| serve:6

Ingredients:

- 1 cup double zero flour
- 4 egg yolk
- 1tsp kosher salt
- Filling ingredients
- 1 whole chicken
- Smoky seasoning
- pint ricotta
- 1 Tbsp salt
- 1 tsp black pepper
- 1/2 Tbsp crushed red pepper
- 1 Tbsp lemon juice
- Sauce ingredients
- 2 Tbsp butter
- 1 calabrese pepper
- 2 large basil leaves

Directions:

1. Set the Grill for direct cooking at 300°F with 1 cup smoking chips
2. In a mixing bowl, add flour, salt, and egg yolk. Mix until the dough comes together, set to rest for 30 minutes.
3. For the filling, apply your Smokey seasoning to all sides of the chicken. Place on the Grill and roast for 2 hours. Remove and allow to cool. Shred the chicken and mix with the filling ingredients.
4. Roll out the pasta dough into thin sheets, place fillings in 1 oz. ball onto one of the sheets, about 1.5 meters apart. Wet the sheet around the filling with water, place a second sheet over the first one, and press down to seal the ravioli. Using a pizza cutter, cut the ravioli into squares. Cook the pasta for about 4 minutes. Reserve 1 ounce of pasta water
5. For the sauce, add 1 Tbsp of butter and Calabrese chili in a cast-iron skillet, cook the butter until it is brown; add 1 oz. of the pasta water, and the cooked ravioli. Cook for 1 minute. Remove from Grill and stir in the remaining butter and basil leaves.

Smoked Bourbon Chilli

Prep time: 15 minutes | Cook time: 3 hours 45 minutes | Serves: 4

Ingredients:

- 4 Tbsp extra virgin olive oil
- 2 lbs. ground sirloin
- 2 onions diced
- 1 green bell pepper, chopped
- 1 Tbsp ground cumin
- 1 tsp cocoa powder
- 1 Tbsp brown sugar
- 1 tsp ground cinnamon
- 1 tsp dried oregano
- 1lb Italian sausage
- 1 (15 oz.) can of kidney bean drained
- 2 serrano chile, chopped
- 4 garlic cloves, chopped
- 1 can crushed tomatoes with liquid
- 1 red bell pepper, diced
- 3 Tbsp chili powder
- 1 (15 oz.) can of chili beans
- 1 (15 oz.) can white beans drained
- 2 jalapeno chile, chopped
- 1 Tbsp ancho powder
- 2 Tbsp Tobasco sauce
- 3 Tbsp ancho chili and seasoning
- 1 cup red wine
- 2 oz. bourbon
- 2 cups beef broth
- 2 bay leaves
- 2 dried ancho chili peppers

Directions:

1. Set Grill for indirect cooking with Plate Setter at 350^{0}F with 3 chunks of wood
2. Place a cast-iron Dutch oven on the Grill and add olive oil, heat for a few minutes. Add the ground sirloin and sausage and stir to break up the meat into small pieces. Cook for 1 hour, stirring occasionally. Remove and drain the meat and set aside.
3. Return the Dutch oven to the Grill, add 2 more Tbsp of olive oil, add green and red peppers, jalapenos, and serrano peppers, and sauté for 10 minutes. Add garlic and cook for another 3 minutes.
4. Add the remaining ingredients and the meat. Cook uncovered for 3 hours.
5. Remove the bay leaves and dried Chile.

Smoked Brisket

Prep time: 15 minutes | Cook time: 12 hours | Serves: 8

Ingredients:

- 8 lb brisket
- 1/4 cup of paprika
- 1 cup of salt
- 1/4 cup garlic powder
- 1 cup ground black pepper
- 1/4 cup ground white pepper
- 1/4 cup ground mustard
- 1/4 cup white sugar

Directions:

1. Set the Grill for indirect using the Plate Setter at 275^{0}F, add soaked oak.
2. Trim excess fat off the brisket. Mix all the ingredients and rub on the brisket.
3. Cook the brisket until the internal temperature is 203^{0}F. This usually takes about 10 hours. Serve.

Smoked Beef Birria

Prep time: 3 hours | Cook time: 8 hours | Serves: 7

Ingredients:

- 8 lbs beef short ribs
- Adobo ingredients
- 8 guajillo chiles
- 10 cloves of garlic
- 5 ancho chiles
- 2 medium onions
- 1/2 oz. ginger
- 2 cups of water

- 2 tsp freshly ground black pepper
- 1/2 tsp ground cloves
- 1/2 tsp oregano
- 4 bay leaves
- 8 sprigs thyme
- 1/2 tsp ground cinnamon
- 3 tsp salt
- 4 Tbsp vinegar

Directions:

1. Set the Grill for indirect cooking at 350^{0}F
2. In a Dutch oven, cook Chile, garlic ginger, onions, and water. Cook until Chile is tender, drain the water, and blend with the rest of the adobo ingredients.
3. Clean and marinate the ribs in 1/2 of the adobo mix for 3 hours. Place on the grid and smoke for 4 hours. Remove the rib and place in a Dutch oven, add the remaining adobo mix. Cook for another 4 hours

Chimichurri Smoked Chicken Salad Sandwich

Prep time: 2 hours | Cook time: 30 minutes | Serves: 2

Ingredients:

- 2 chicken breast
- 2 Tbsp olive oil
- 1/2 Tbsp garlic salt
- Applewood chips (soaked)
- 2 toasted onion rolls
- Smoked chicken salad ingredients
- 2 smoked chicken breast chopped
- 1 tsp chimichurri
- 2 Tbsp mayo
- 1 Tbsp chopped peppadews
- Salt and lime to taste

Directions:

1. In a Ziploc bag, add chicken and garlic salt and olive oil. Allow to rest for two hours.
2. Placed a handful of soaked apple chips in the Grill, set the temperature to 340^{0}F. Add your chicken and smoke for 30 minutes, remove from heat, and allow to cool.
3. In a large bowl, add mayo and chimichurri to a medium-sized bowl, stir and combine. Add chopped chicken, grilled corn, peppadews, salt, and lime. Mix and set aside
4. Toast onion rolls on Grill for few minutes and fill with chicken salad.

Smoked Brisket Roll

Prep time: 10 minutes | Cook time: 4 hours | Serves: 4

Ingredients:

- 6lbs. brisket
- 1 cup brisket rub
- 1/2 bag Jack Daniel wood chip soaked in cold water
- Bardough House slaw
- Salted farm butter
- 4 country loaf rolls

Directions:

1. Coat the brisket on all side with an even layer of rub and allow to rest for 1 hour
2. Set the Grill for indirect cooking at 225^{0}F.
3. Place the brisket on the grid with the fat side up, smoke for 8 hours until it reaches an internal temperature of 200^{0}F. Remove and place on a rimmed baking sheet and allow to rest for 30 minutes
4. Cut the brisket in thin slices. Cut the rolls in half, butter on both sides, add brisket and slaw.

Smoked Apples

Prep time: 10 minutes | Cook time: 1 hour 30min | Serves: 6

Ingredients:

- 6 big apples
- 6 Tbsp unsalted butter
- 1/4 cup brown sugar
- 1/4 cup dried currants
- 1/4 cup shortbread crumbs
- 1/2 tsp ground cinnamon
- 1/4 tsp freshly grated nutmeg
- 1 tsp vanilla extract
- 4 whole cinnamon sticks
- 4 marshmallows (halved)
- Vanilla ice-cream

Directions:

1. Core the apple using apple corer; make sure you create a cavity for stuffing.
2. In a bowl, cream butter and sugar until fluffy. Add the currants, crumbs, cinnamon, nutmeg, and vanilla. Spoon the mixture into the apple, stick in a cinnamon stick through the filling, and place the half marshmallow on top.
3. Arrange the apples on the grilling rings, preheat the Grill to 300°F. Smoke the apple for 1 hour or until sides are squeezably soft and not collapsing.
4. Serve with ice-cream

Smoked Planked Trout

Prep time: 10 minutes | Cook time: 30minutes | Serves: 4

Ingredients:

- 4 whole trout (12-16oz.)
- 16 whole fresh basil leaves
- 2 Tbsp cold unsalted butter
- 5 lemon sliced and seeded
- 8 thin slices pancetta
- Sea salt
- Freshly ground black pepper

Directions:

1. Preheat the Grill to 450°F, grill the plank for about 2 minutes per side. Allow to cool
2. Rinse the trout and blot dry, season with salt and pepper. Place 4 basil leaves, lemon slice and butter slice in the cavity of each trout. Tie two pieces of pancetta to each trout (one on top and the other at the bottom) and secure with a butcher's string.
3. Arrange the trout on the plank with half lemon on each plank.
4. Smoke-roast the trout for 20 minutes or until the pancetta is sizzling, crispy, and the trout is cooked through.
5. Serve hot.

Chapter 9: Braising Recipes

Beer-Braised Pork Shank

Prep Time and Cooking Time: 23 minutes
|Serves:6

Ingredients To Use:

- 2 Tbsp Flour
- Kosher salt
- Ground black pepper
- 2 Tbsp olive oil
- 2 Tbsp butter
- 1 medium onion, diced
- 2 carrots, trimmed and diced
- 1 Tbsp garlic, minced
- 1 cup dried mushrooms
- 2 cup beef broth
- 2 Tsp chili powder
- 2 thyme sprigs
- 2 Tsp coffee, instant
- 1 Tbsp Worcestershire sauce
- 12 oz dark beer, porter
- 2 dried bay leaves

Step-by-Step Directions:

1. Preheat Smoker-grill to 300°F with the cover of the grill closed for 10 minutes.
2. Hold pork shank together with a butcher string and sprinkle pepper and salt over it.
3. Place a Dutch oven on the cooking grid. Add oil and pork shanks. Cook shank until brown on both sides.
4. Remove shanks from heat and transfer to a plate.
5. Sauté onions, carrots, and garlic in Dutch oven until tender, about 8 minutes.
6. Mix in beef broth, beer, and Worcestershire sauce to the sautéed vegetables. Increase the temperature and bring to boil. Allow simmering at Medium temperature until one-third of the liquid is gone.
7. Add tomato paste, coffee, thyme, chili powder, and bay leaves.
8. Transfer pork shanks from the plate into the Dutch oven and scoop sauce atop it.
9. Cook shanks until tender, about 3 hours.
10. Combine in a bowl, butter, and flour. Add the flour mixture in the last hour to thicken the sauce.
11. Take out bay leaves and thyme springs. Cut out butcher's string. Serve pork shank with gravy atop it and garnish with parsley.

Beef Pot Roast

Prep Time and Cooking time: 3 hours 10 minutes | Serves: 6

Ingredients To Use:

- 3 cup beef stock
- 1 cup carrots, chopped
- 1 Tbsp garlic, minced
- 1/4 cup softened butter
- 1 Tsp ground black pepper
- 2 red onions, chopped
- 4lb chuck roast
- 1 Tbsp kosher salt
- 1Tbsp sage, chopped
- 1/2 cup red wine

Step-by-Step Directions:

1. Preheat Grill & Smoker to 300°F with the cover of the grill closed for 10 minutes.
2. In a stockpot, put in red wine, beef stock,

butter, garlic, carrot, red onion, sage, and chuck roast—season with pepper and salt. Stir the contents and cover the pot.

3. Transfer stockpot to the preheated grill; close the grill lid and leave to cook for 3 hours, until the roast reaches an internal temperature of 203°F.

4. Serve.

Butter-Braised Springs Onions with Lots of Chives

Prep Time and Cooking Time: 25minutes|Serves:3

- 1lb spring onions, trimmed
- Kosher salt
- 1/4 tsp chives, chopped
- 4 Tbsp unsalted butter

Step-by-Step Directions:

1. In a large skillet, add onions, 1/2 cup water, two tablespoons butter and sprinkle in the salt. Cover skillet and bring to a boil. Reduce heat and simmer onion until almost tender, about 15 minutes. Remove cover, stir continuously and leave onions to cook for another 5 minutes, until fork-tender.

2. Take out onions and place them on a plate. Heat the liquid in skillet until it reduces to about two teaspoons, then add the remaining butter. Transfer onions to the skillet and stir it in with the sauce. Garnish with chives.

Rosemary Braised Lamb Shank

Prep Time and Cooking Time: 2 hours 45 minutes | Serves:4

Ingredients To Use:

- 2 spring's rosemary
- 2 celery stalk
- 3 garlic clove, minced
- 2 cups red wine
- 2 carrots, diced
- 4 lamb shanks, fat trimmed
- 2 Tbsp olive oil
- 2 Tbsp chophouse steak
- 2 onion, diced

Step-by-Step Directions:

1. Preheat Smoker-grill to 350°F.
2. Brush oil over lamb shanks, arrange on grill and grill on each side until brown, about 2 minutes.
3. Transfer the shanks from grill to a heatproof baking pan; add onions, carrots, garlic, onions, rosemary springs, beef stock, red wine, and Chophouse steaks.
4. Reduce grill temperature to 325°F
5. Cover baking pan with aluminum foil and place on grill.
6. Braise the shanks for 2-1/2 hours on smoker-grill, until tender.

Korean BBQ Short Ribs

Prep Time and Cooking Time: 5 hours 40 minutes | Serves:4

Ingredients To Use:

- 1 cup beef broth
- 1 Tsp ginger, minced
- 1/2 cup of soy sauce
- 1 Tsp toasted sesame seeds
- 6 beef short ribs, membrane removed
- 2 Tbsp brown sugar
- 1 Tbsp beef rub
- 2 garlic cloves, minced
- 1 Tbsp sriracha sauce

Step-by-Step Directions:

1. Preheat Smoker-grill to 250°F.
2. Combine in a medium bowl, brown sugar,

garlic, ginger, beef broth, soy sauce, sriracha, sesame, beef, and brisket rub, and then set aside.

3. Place ribs in a baking dish and add the marinade. Cover and leave to marinate in a refrigerator for about 6-12hours.
4. Transfer marinated short rib to the top of the grill grate. Grill for 4 hours; rub leftover marinade juice on the rib occasionally.
5. Remove rib from the grill and leave to rest on a platter for 15minutes. Serve.

Red Wine Braised Short Ribs

Prep Time and Cooking Time: 9 hours | Serves: 12

Ingredients To Use:

- Kosher salt
- 1/2 cup onion, thinly sliced
- 4 garlic cloves, smashed
- 5lb brisket, flat-cut
- 2 Tbsp olive oil
- 2 bay leaves
- 6 spring's thyme
- 28 oz of canned whole tomatoes
- 4 medium carrots cut lengthwise
- 750ml red wine
- 1 Tbsp tomato paste

Step-by-Step Directions:

1. Preheat Smoker-grill to 350°F.
2. Place brisket on a flat surface and sprinkle pepper and salt on it.
3. Pour oil into a large ovenproof pot and cook the brisket in it for about 10 minutes or until meat browns. Remove brisket and place on a plate, then discard fat in the pot.
4. Add onions, garlic, thyme, bay leaves, tomatoes, wine, tomato paste, celery, salt, and pepper in a large pot. Return

brisket to pot, fat side up, and then cover the pot. Braise brisket on the grill for about 3hours, until fork tender.
5. Place carrot on brisket, then cook until carrot is tender and braising liquid in the pot is concentrated. It will take about 30 minutes.
6. Remove fat from the sauce—transfer brisket and braising liquid to a bowl. Cover and leave to rest for at least 4 hours.
7. When ready to serve, preheat grill to 325°F. Heat braising liquid and brisket for about 1 hour.

Pork Carnitas

Prep Time and Cooking Time: 3 hours | Serves: 6

Ingredients To Use:

- Lime wedges
- 3 jalapeno pepper, minced
- A handful of cilantro, chopped
- 1 cup of chicken broth
- 2 Tbsp olive oil
- Corn tortilla
- 3lb pork shoulder, cut into cubes
- Queso Fresco, crumbled
- 2 Tbsp pork rubs

Step-by-Step Directions:

1. Preheat Smoker-grill to 300°F.
2. Mop the rub over the pork shoulder. Place pork shoulder in a cast-iron Dutch oven and pour in chicken broth. Transfer pot to grill grate and cook 2½ hours, until fork tender.
3. Remove the cover, bring to a boil then reduce the liquid in pot by half. All this happens within 15 minutes.
4. Place a tablespoon of bacon fat on the skillet and fry the pork for about 10

minutes, until crisp.

5. Take out pork and serve with cilantro, jalapeno, lime, queso fresco, and corn tortillas.

Belgian Ale-Braised Brisket

Prep and Cooking Time: 3 hours | Serves: 6

Ingredients To Use:

- 1/4 cup Dijon mustard
- 2 bay leaves
- 1/4 cup all-purpose flour
- 1/4 cup dark brown sugar, packed
- 2 Tbsp bacon fat
- 2 medium onion, thinly sliced
- Kosher salt
- 4lb beef brisket, flat cut, untrimmed
- 1 Tbsp grated ginger
- 4 cups beef broth
- 750ml bottle Belgian style tripel ale

Step-by-Step Directions:

1. Preheat Smoker-grill to 400ºF.
2. Rub brisket in salt and leave in a reusable plastic bag for 8 hours at room temperature.
3. In a small bowl, mix ginger, brown sugar, and ginger.
4. Remove brisket from the bag, rub mustard over brisket, and place on the grill grate. Roast for 40 minutes, until the top, is brown.
5. Transfer brisket to a plate and set aside.
6. Reduce the temperature of the grill to 300ºF.
7. Heat bacon fat in a cast-iron Dutch oven placed on the grill. Add onions and sprinkle in the salt. Stir continuously and cook until brown, about 10 minutes.
8. Reduce heat and stir in flour and cook for another 4 minutes. Add ale, bay leaves, and stock, and then allow to simmer. Put in brisket and cover the lid of the Dutch oven.
9. Braise brisket for 4 hours with the grill cover closed.
10. Remove bay leaves and place brisket on a platter. Allow resting of brisket for 20 minutes before carving.
11. Serve brisket with braising liquid.

Bourbon Braised Beef Short Ribs

Prep Time and Cooking Time: 3 hours 15 minutes | Serves:6

Ingredients To Use:

- 2 Tbsp Worcestershire sauce
- 3 Tbsp soy sauce
- 2 Tbsp bourbon
- 1/2 cup Dijon mustard
- 1 cup beef stock
- 12 beef short ribs

Step-by-Step Directions:

1. Preheat Smoker-grill to 250ºF, with the lid closed for about 15 minutes
2. Mix the Worcestershire sauce, mustard, and molasses.
3. Brush sauce on each side of the rib.
4. Prepare the mop sauce by mixing the soy sauce, beef stock, and bourbon in a food-safe plastic spray bottle.
5. Arrange the ribs directly on the grill and braise for 2 hours, until an internal temperature of 165ºF is reached. Spray the mop sauce over the rib occasionally for tender perfection.
6. Remove rib from the grill and place on an aluminum foil. Pour remaining mop sauce over the ribs and wrap the foil over the ribs.
7. Transfer foil enclosed rib for direct cooking to the grill grate. Braise the ribs until the Instant read thermometer

reads a temperature of 195°F, about one hour.

8. Remove foil enclosed rib from grill and place on a platter to rest for 15 minutes
9. Take out ribs from foil and serve.

Veal Paprikash

Prep Time and Cooking Time: 1 hour 25 minutes | Serves: 6

Ingredients To Use:

- 3lb Veal, cut into 1-inch piece
- 1 yellow onion, chopped
- 1 tsp cayenne pepper
- 1 small red pepper, finely chopped
- Kosher salt
- 1 cup regular sour cream
- 1 Tsp all-purpose flour
- 1 medium ripe tomato
- 1 Tsp paprika
- 2 Tbsp vegetable oil
- 2 Tbsp butter

Step-by-Step Directions:

1. Preheat Smoker-grill to 350°F, with the lid closed for about 15 minutes
2. Heat oil and melt butter in a Dutch oven, add the onion and cook until tender, about 3 minutes.
3. Add veal, and then season onion with paprika and cayenne pepper. Cover the lid of the Dutch oven and allow the meat to cook for about 10 minutes.
4. Add tomato, bell pepper, and season with salt. Stir and leave to cook for 45 minutes, until tender.
5. Combine the flour and sour cream in a small bowl. Stir in the flour mixture into the Dutch oven and cook for another 10 minutes.
6. Remove pot from the cooking grid and enjoy the dish.

Red Wine Beef Stew

Prep Time and Cooking Time: 3 hours 30 minutes | Serves: 8

Ingredients To Use:

- 1-1/2 tsp kosher salt
- 4lb chuck roast, cut into 2-inch pieces
- 1 Tsp ground black pepper
- 1/4 cup tomato paste
- 1 Tsp olive oil
- 2 cups dry red wine
- 2 bay leaves
- 4 spring's fresh thyme
- 2 lb carrots, peeled and chopped
- 1lb red potatoes, cut into half
- 4 cups chicken broth
- 3 Tsp all-purpose flour

Step-by-Step Directions:

1. Preheat Smoker-grill to 325°F, with the lid closed for about 15 minutes
2. Place meat in a bowl and sprinkle in salt, pepper, and flour. Toss together until meat is adequately seasoned.
3. Heat oil in a cast-iron Dutch oven and cook the meat at *Medium* for about 8 minutes, until brown.
4. Remove meat and place on a plate. Add wine, broth, tomato paste, thyme, bay leaves, and 1/4 of carrots into the Dutch oven and bring to a boil. Transfer meat to Dutch oven and place on the grill grate for direct cooking. Cook meat for about 2 hours.
5. Remove cooked vegetables from Dutch oven and add remaining carrots and potatoes. Cook until meat is fork-tender, about 1 hour. Serve.

Pear Braised Pork Tenderloin

Prep time: 30 minutes | Cook time: 45 minutes | Serves: 4

Ingredients:

- 1-1/2 pound pork tenderloin, halved
- 1/2 cup dry white wine
- 3/4 cup olive oil
- 1 clove garlic, minced
- 1/2 tsp rosemary
- 1 tsp sea salt
- 5 pearl onions, finely chopped
- 1 pear, cored and chopped
- 1 tsp granulated mixed peppercorns

Directions:

1. Set your Grill to direct cooking with the Plate Setter at 400^{0}F
2. In a bowl, add the pear, white wine, olive oil, rosemary, and garlic. Mash the ingredients together. Season the pork with pepper and salt and placed it in a drip pan.
3. Pour the pear mixture on the pork and garnish with onions, cover the drip pan with foil.
4. Cook for 45 minutes or until internal temperature is 145^{0}F

Mushroom Pork Chops

Prep time: 10 minutes | Cook time: 30 minutes | Serves: 4

Ingredients:

- 4 pork chops
- 1 onion chopped
- 1 pinch garlic salt
- 1/2 lb. fresh mushroom 9sliced)
- 1 can of condensed cream
- Salt and pepper to taste

Directions:

1. Set the Grill to direct cooking with the Plate Setter at 400^{0}F
2. Season your pork with salt, pepper, and garlic to taste. Brown the pork chops in a large skillet

3. Sauté onions and mushroom for 1min add the cream and stir together. Pour the cream mixture over the pork chop. Reset the Grill to indirect cooking with Plate Setter at 300^{0}F and simmer for 20 minutes or until chops are cooked through.

Rosemary Braised Lamb Shanks

Prep time: 30minutes | Cook time: 2 hours | Serves: 6

Ingredients:

- 6 lamb shanks
- 1 bottle red wine
- 1 can condensed chicken broth
- 10 cloves garlic, minced
- 1 can of whole peeled tomato juice
- 1 can beef broth
- 2 Tbsp olive oil
- 2 onions, chopped
- 3 large carrots, cut into 1/4 inch rounds
- 5 tsp chopped fresh rosemary
- 2 tsp chopped fresh thyme
- Salt and pepper to taste

Directions:

1. Set Grill to direct cooking at 400^{0}F
2. In a pot, add onions, carrots, and garlic and sauté for 10minutes or until golden brown, stir in the wine, tomato broth, and chicken broth. Season with rosemary and thyme. Submerge the shank in the broth and bring it to a boil.
3. Reset the Grill to indirect cooking with the Plate Setter at 290^{0}F. Cover and simmer for 2 hours, remove the lid and simmer for 20 minutes. Remove the lamb shank, boil the juice until thickened.
4. Serve with the lamb shank.

Skillet-Braised Brussels Sprouts

Prep time: 15 minutes | Cook time: 25 minutes | Serves: 4

Ingredients:

- 4 beacon (about 1/4 inches thick)
- 1 pound Brussels sprout (trimmed and sliced)
- 1 Tbsp balsamic vinegar
- 1 Tbsp butter
- 1/2 cup chicken stock
- 1 clove garlic (sliced)
- Salt and black pepper (to taste)

Directions:

1. Set the Grill to direct cooking at 300°F
2. Place bacon in a large skillet and cook for 10 minutes or until crisp. Remove bacon from skillet, leaving the grease behind. Increase the Grill temperature to 400°F, sauté the Brussels sprouts in the bacon grease for 3 minutes or until slightly brown, add garlic, and sauté for 1 minute.
3. Pour chicken broth over Brussel mixture and cover the skillet. Reduce the Grill temperature and allow it to simmer for 5 minutes or until Brussels sprout is green. Remove the lid and continue to simmer until the liquid is evaporated. Remove skillet from heat and stir in beacon, butter, salt, pepper, and vinegar. Serve.

Jewish Style Sweet and Sour Brisket

Prep time: 15 minutes | Cook time: 2 hours 45 minutes | Serves: 8

Ingredients:

- 4 pounds beef brisket
- 3/4 cup brown sugar
- 1/2 cup of rice vinegar
- 1 clove garlic, finely chopped

- 1 cup ketchup
- 1 cup of water
- 1 Tbsp salt

Directions:

1. Set the Grill to direct cooking at 400°F
2. Heat the brisket in a dutch oven until it is brown on both sides, then stir in the vinegar, water, salt, ketchup, brown sugar, onions, garlic, and vinegar. Bring to boil and reduce the heat. Simmer for 2 hours 30 minutes until brisket is tender.
3. Discard brisket and cool before carving. Put in a large platter, pour gravy on top, and keep in the fridge overnight.
4. Reheat when ready to serve.

Orange and Milk Braised Pork Carnitas

Prep time: 10 minutes | Cook time: 2 hours 30 minutes | Serves: 8

Ingredients:

- 3-1/2 boneless pork shoulder Cut into large pieces)
- 1 orange (zested and juiced)
- 2 cups whole milk
- 1 Tbsp freshly ground black pepper
- 2 bay leaves
- 2 tsp cumin
- 1 Tbsp kosher salt
- 2 Tbsp vegetable oil
- 1 tsp dried oregano
- 1/4 tsp cayenne pepper

Directions:

1. Set the Grill to direct heat at 400°F
2. Season pork with salt and pepper. Heat oil in a big pot; cook the pork in oil for 5 minutes or until brown.
3. Season pork with bay leaves, oregano, cayenne pepper, stir in fresh orange

juice, orange zest, and milk. Bring mixture to boil and reduce the heat. Cover and simmer until meat is fork-tender. Remove from heat.

4. Set the Grill to indirect cooking with the plate setter at 450⁰F. Place the baking stone on the Grill grid, remove pork from the liquid. Grease the baking pan with fat from the liquid and transfer the pork to the baking pan. Drizzle 2 Tbsp of floating fat on the pork, season with salt.

5. Bake for 15minutes or until brown or crisp

Mushroom Chicken Piccata

Prep time: 20 minutes | Cook time: 30 minutes | Serves: 6

Ingredients:

- 1/2 cup of all-purpose flour
- 1/2 tsp paprika
- 1 egg
- 1 tsp salt
- 6 skinless boneless chicken breast (halved)
- 1/2 pound of freshly sliced mushroom
- 2 Tbsp milk
- 4 Tbsp butter
- 1/4 cup chopped onion
- 1 cup chicken broth
- 2 Tbsp lemon juice
- 1/2 cup of white wine
- 1 Tbsp chopped fresh parsley
- 1 Tbsp corn starch

Directions:

1. Set the Grill to direct cooking using a plate setter at 400⁰F
2. In one bowl, mix flour, salt, and paprika. In another bowl, combine egg and milk. Dip the pieces of chicken in the mixture of egg and milk before the seasoned

flour. Set aside.

3. In a large skillet, heat butter and add the chicken pieces. Sauté until golden brown, add your onions and mushroom and sauté for another 3 minutes.

4. In a large bowl, add broth, wine, lemon juice, and corn starch. Mix well together, pour the mixture over the chicken and mushroom. Reduce the heat and allow the mixture to simmer for 25 minutes until well cooked. Sprinkle with parsley and serve.

Short Ribs Braised with Mushrooms and Tomatoes

Prep time: 15 minutes | Cook time: 2 hours15minutes | Serves: 8

Ingredients:

- 1/2 cup porcini mushroom, dried
- 1 onion sliced
- 1/2 cup of water
- 2 cloves garlic, chopped
- 2-1/2 pounds of beef short ribs
- 2 cups beef broth
- 1 bay leave
- 1 pinch cayenne pepper
- 1 cup of tomato sauce
- 2 Tbsp vegetable oil
- 1 tsp dried rosemary
- Salt and freshly ground pepper to taste.

Directions:

1. Set the Grill to indirect cooking at 300⁰F
2. In a bowl, soak the mushroom for 30minutes until they are rehydrated, drain and reserve the liquid. Dice the mushroom.
3. Mix salt and black pepper to form a rub and use to season both sides of the ribs. Add vegetable oil to skillet placed over medium-high heat, then cook the rib in

the hot oil for 12 minutes or until it is brown. Remove from heat and set in a baking pan and transfer to the Dutch oven

4. Return the skillet to heat, add onions and a dash of salt, sauté until it is soft. Add garlic, then sauté for another 1 minute. Stir the mushroom into the onion mixture and add the reserved mushroom liquid

5. Bring the mixture to boil, stir in the beef broth, rosemary, tomato sauce, salt, bay leaf, and cayenne pepper. Pour the tomato mixture over the rib in the baking pan.

6. Cook the ribs in the Grill for 2 hours or until fork-tender.

Stuffed Cabbage Rolls

Prep time: 20 minutes | Cook time: 40 minutes | Serves: 6

Ingredients:

- 8 cabbage leaves
- 1/3 cup of cooked rice
- 1lb ground beef
- 1/4 cup of chopped onions
- 1/2 tsp freshly pepper
- 1 tsp of salt
- 1 can of tomato soup
- 2/3 cup of water
- 1 egg, slightly whisked

Directions:

1. Set your Grill for indirect cooking with the plate setter at 300^{0}F

2. In a large saucepan, add water and salt. Bring the water to a boil, stir in cabbage leaves, then cook for 3 minutes or until soft. Drain.

3. In a bowl, thoroughly mix ground beef, cooked rice, salt, onion, egg, 2 Tbsp of

tomato soup, and pepper. Divide the mix equally on the cabbage leaves. Roll the leaves and secure with toothpicks.

4. In large skillet, arrange cabbage rolls and pour leftover tomato soup on it. Place on the Grill grid and bring to a boil, lower heat, and simmer for 40 minutes.

Green Coconut Chicken

Prep time: 25 minutes | Cook time: 1 hour 25 minutes | Serves: 4

Ingredients:

- 1/2 bunch green onions chopped (white and light green part only)
- 4 chicken legs
- 2 Tbsp of vegetable oil
- 1-1/2 cups 1-inch eggplants chunks
- 6 slices fresh ginger
- 1-3/4 cups water
- 1 can of coconut milk
- 6 cloves garlic, minced
- 3 seeded jalapeno peppers, finely chopped
- 1 handful of cilantro
- 1 onion, finely sliced
- 1 Tbsp curry powder
- 2 Tbsp fish sauce
- 2 Tbsp lime juice
- 1 Tbsp brown sugar
- 1 handful of basil leaves
- 2 cups of 1-inch diced sweet potatoes
- salt and freshly ground black pepper, as desired

Directions:

1. Set the Grill to indirect cooking using the Plate Setter at 390^{0}F

2. Season the chicken legs with salt. Heat vegetable oil in Dutch Oven, add the chicken and cook 4 minutes per side, or until it turns golden brown. Remove

chicken from Dutch Oven, then set aside.

3. Add coconut milk, garlic, water, pepper, cilantro, jalapeno, and green onions in a blender. Blend until smooth.

4. Sizzle 1 Tbsp of vegetable oil in the Dutch oven, stir in ginger and onions. Cook for 1-2 minutes or until sizzling. Sprinkle curry over ginger and onions, cook and stir for 1 minute or until lightly toasted. Add the chicken leg, coconut mixture, brown sugar, fish sauce, and lime juice. Bring the mixture to boil and reduce the heat. Cover and allow to simmer, skim off fats, and cook for 45 minutes or until legs are soft.

5. Remove the chicken from the mixture, stir in eggplants and potatoes. Cook for 20minutes or until soft. Stir in basil, season with salt and black pepper as desired. Return the chicken legs to coconut mixture, reduce the heat and allow it to simmer for 5 minutes.

Braised Beef Shank with Wine and Tarragon

Prep time: 15 minutes | Cook time: 5 hours 10 minutes | Serves: 3

Ingredients:

- 2 Tbsp olive oil
- 2 lb. beef shank
- 1 onion (diced)
- 1 pinch of salt and black pepper
- 2 celery stalk diced
- 1 cup marsala wine
- 1 cup of water
- 2 Tbsp of dried tarragon
- 1 can beef broth

Directions:

1. Set the Grill to indirect cooking at 300^{0}F
2. Place an oven-proof Dutch Oven with

the lid over Medium-high heat, add olive oil. Season the beef shank with salt and pepper. Cook the beef shank in hot oil for 5minutes or until browned on all sides. Transfer beef shank to plate

3. Sauté onions and celery in the same Dutch Oven until it is translucent pour wine over the mixture and bring to boil. Return beef shank to the onion-wine mix, add enough water and sprinkle tarragon. Cover with lid.

4. Bake in the Dutch oven for 5 hours. Season with salt and pepper before serving.

Goat Shoulder Braise with Prunes and Preserve Lemons

Prep time: 10minutes | Cook time: 2 hours 20minutes | Serves: 6

Ingredients:

- 3 lbs. goat shoulder
- 1 medium yellow onions (chopped)
- 1/2 cup red wine
- Salt and freshly grounded pepper
- 2 Tbsp olive oil
- 1-1/2 cups of chicken broth
- 1/4 cup chopped Moroccan preserved
- 10 pitted prunes (chopped)

Directions:

1. Set the Grill to direct cooking at 325^{0}F
2. Add oil to heated Dutch oven, then add salt and pepper seasoned goat shoulder. Cook until brown, add onions, and cook for 2-3 minutes. Add the prunes and preserved lemon, then cook for 3 minutes to allow the flavors blend.
3. Pour in the chicken and red wine, then bring to simmer
4. Cover the Dutch oven and bake for 2 hours or until meat is tender.

Chapter 10: Baking Recipes

Banana Walnut bread

Prep Time and Cooking time: 1 hour 15 minutes /Serves: 1

Ingredients To Use:

- 2-1/2 cup of all-purpose flour
- 1 cup of sugar
- 2 eggs
- 1 cup ripe banana, mashed
- 1/4 cup whole milk
- 1/4 cup walnut, finely chopped
- 1 tsp salt
- 3 Tbsp of Vegetable oil
- 3 tsp baking powder

Step-by-Step Directions:

1. Set the Smoker-grill for indirect cooking at 350°F.
2. Combine all the ingredients in a large bowl. Using a mixer (electric or manual), mix the ingredients. Grease and flour the loaf pan. Pour the mixture into the loaf pan.
3. Transfer loaf pan to the grill and cover with steel construction. Bake for 60-75 minutes. Remove and allow to cool.

Peach Blueberry Cobbler

Prep Time and Cooking time: 1hour15 minutes /Serves: 4

Ingredients To Use:

- 2 cups of peaches, peeled and sliced
- 1 cup of fresh blueberries
- 1 cup of all-purpose flour
- 1 cup of milk
- 1/2 cup of melted butter, salted

- 2 tsp Baking powder
- 1-1/2 cup sugar
- 1/2 tsp salt
- 1/2 tsp vanilla extract

Step-by-Step Directions:

1. Set the Smoker-grill to indirect cooking at 375°F
2. In a bowl, add blueberry, peaches, and ¾ cup sugar. Stir the mixture until the blueberry is coated. Set aside.
3. In another bowl, combine the other ingredients with the remaining sugar and mix well. Be careful not to over stir the mixture.
4. Pour into the baking dish, add the blueberry-peach mixture on top. Do not stir.
5. Transfer baking pan to the grill and cover with steel construction. Bake for 45-60 minutes, remove and allow to rest before serving.

Baked Wild Sockeye Salmon

Prep Time and Cooking time: 45 minutes / Serves: 6

Ingredients To Use:

- 6 sockeye salmon fillets
- 3/4 tsp Old bay seasoning
- 1/2 tsp Seafood seasoning.

Step-by-Step Directions:

1. Set the Smoker-grill to indirect cooking at 400°F
2. Rinse the fillet and pat dry with a paper towel. Add the seasoning, then rub all over the fillets.
3. Arrange fillets in a baking dish with the

skin facing down, then transfer the dish to the cooking grid. Cover grill and bake for 15-20 minutes or until fillets begin to flake. Serve.

Pizza dough roll

Prep Time and Cooking time: 1hour 15 minutes | Serves: 6

Ingredients To Use:

- 1 tsp Yeast
- 1 cup of warm water
- 2-1/2 cups of all-purpose flour
- 1 tsp Kosher salt
- Tbsp Virgin olive oil
- 1 tsp Sugar

Step-by-Step Directions:

1. Set the Smoker-grill to indirect cooking at 400^0 F
2. Combine all your ingredients and mix until the mixture is sticky and has a shaggy texture. Knead the dough for 3-5 minutes, then set aside and cover. Keep for 1 hour at room temperature or until it doubles in size.
3. Divide the dough into six equal parts and roll into a ball using a floured hand. Cover the baking pan with a parchment paper, place the roll on it, then cover and allow to rise for 30 minutes. Transfer the baking pan to the cooking grid, then cover.
4. Bake for 15-20min or until the rolls are golden brown. Allow to cool before serving.

Take and Bake Pepperoni Pizza

Prep Time and Cooking time: 15 minutes | Serves: 4

Ingredients To Use:

- Take and bake pizza bread

- Pepperoni toppings of your choice

Step-by-Step Directions:

1. Set the Smoker-grill to indirect cooking at 400^0 F
2. If refrigerated, remove pizza bread from the refrigerator 20-30 minutes before baking. Add the toppings and place the bread directly on the cooking grates for a crispier crust.
3. Bake for 10-15 minutes. Remove pizza with a pizza paddle, and allow to cool before cutting into sclices and serving.

Classic Apple Pie

Prep Time and Cooking time: 2 hours | Serves: 8

Ingredients To Use:

- 2 Tbsp all-purpose flour
- 2 pie dough rounds
- 6 cups of apple, peeled and sliced
- 1 Tbsp lemon juice
- 3/4 cup of sugar
- 1/4 tsp powdered nutmeg
- 1/2 tsp powdered cinnamon
- 1/2 tsp salt

Step-by-Step Directions:

1. Set the Smoker-grill to indirect cooking at 425^0 F
2. In a large bowl, combine all your ingredients (except for the pie dough) and mix well. Gently press one of the pie dough unto a 10-inch pie dough plate. Make sure it is firm and covers the sides.
3. Pour in your apple mixture. Cover the filling with the second pie dough, gently clip the two doughs together. Make a crosshatch slit on the top with a knife—transfer dough plate to the cooking grid.
4. Bake for 45-60 minutes or until the crust browns. Allow to cool for 1 hour before

serving.

Red Chile and Lime Shortbread Cookies

Prep Time and Cooking time: 30 minutes | Serves: 8

Ingredients To Use:

- 2 tsp lime zest
- 8 Tbsp unsalted butter
- 1 cup of all-purpose flour
- 1/2 tsp Salt
- 1 tsp Red Chile rub
- 1/4 cup of sugar

Step-by-Step Directions:

1. Set the Smoker-grill to indirect cooking at 300^0 F
2. In a large bowl, combine all the ingredients (except flour). Mix thoroughly until the butter is creamy but not smooth. Gradually add the flour until it forms a ball.
3. Transfer the dough onto a floured surface, roll until about 1/4-inches thick. Cut into eight equal parts, but do not cut through.
4. Arrange in a cake pan, bake for 10 minutes. Allow to cool before serving.

Kahluá Coffee Brownies

Prep Time and Cooking time: 60 minutes | Serves: 12

Ingredients To Use:

- 4 oz. pure chocolate, unsweetened
- 1 cup of white chocolate chip
- 1 cup of bittersweet chocolate chip
- 4 eggs
- 1/8 Tsp of salt
- Tbsp instant coffee
- 1-1/2 cup all-purpose flour
- cups of sugar
- 1 cup unsalted butter

Step-by-Step Directions:

1. Set the Smoker-grill to indirect cooking at 350^0 F
2. Place a small pot on the cooking grid, then add the butter and coffee. Stir until it melts completely. Remove the pot from heat and stir in the unsweetened chocolate, stir until it is smooth. Add the eggs one at a time, mix well. While still mixing, add the sugar, flour, and salt. Gently fold the white chocolate and bittersweet chocolate into the mixture.
3. Pour the mixture into a baking pan and bake on the grates for 20 minutes or until a toothpick comes out clean.
4. Remove and allow to cool.

Twice- Baked potatoes with Smoked Gouda and grilled scallions

Prep Time and Cooking time: 1hours 15 minutes | Serves: 6

Ingredients To Use:

- 3 large potatoes
- 8 TbspUnsalted butter
- Tbsp Of barbeque rub
- 1-1/2 cup of smoked gouda cheese (grated)
- 1/4 cup of extra-virgin olive oil
- 3/4 cup heavy cream
- Salt and pepper to taste
- 1/4 cup chopped scallions

Step-by-Step Directions:

1. Set the Smoker-grill to indirect cooking at 400^0 F
2. Brush the potatoes with olive oil, make incisions with fork and season with salt.

Wrap with aluminum foil paper and bake on grill grates for 30 minutes per side. Transfer to a rimmed sheet and allow to cool.

3. Cut the potatoes lengthwise, scoop out the flesh into a bowl. Add butter and 1 cup of cheese. Set aside. Place a small pot over low-medium heat, add cream, then heat for 1 minute. Add the scallions and the barbeque rub and mix well

4. Add the scallion mixture to the potatoes and cheese in the bowl, combine until it is evenly mixed. Scoop the mixture back into the potato shell and top with cheese.

5. Bake for 5 minutes or until the cheese melts.

Chocolate Pecan Bourbon Pie

Prep Time and Cooking time: 60 minutes | Serves: 6

Ingredients To Use:

- 1/4 cup bourbon
- 1 cup semisweet chocolate chips
- 1 cup of dark corn syrup
- Tbsp of melted unsalted butter
- 3 large egg (beaten)
- 1 cup of pecan (chopped)
- 1 cup of brown sugar
- 1 pie shell

Step-by-Step Directions:

1. Set the Smoker-grill to indirect cooking at 400°F

2. In a bowl, combine the corn syrup, egg, butter, sugar, and bourbon. Then add the chocolate chips and mix well. Pour the filling into the pie shell.

3. Place the pie plates on the grid and bake for 45 minutes or until fillings turn brown.

4. Remove and allow to cool. Refrigerate or serve.

Mediterranean Bread

Prep time: 2 hours 30 minutes | Cook time: 50 minutes | serves: 8

Ingredients:

- 1/2 cup plus 2 cups of evaporated milk
- 6 Tbsp of condensed milk
- 2-1/2 tsp of nutritional yeast
- 6 cups of bread flour
- 6 Tbsp of melted, unsalted butter
- 1 Tbsp of table salt
- 1 large egg
- 2 Tbsp of water plus olive oil
- 1/4 cup plus 1/4 cup black olive tapenade
- 4 roasted red bell pepper,
- 2 cups of grated Parmigiano-Reggiano cheese.

Directions:

1. Set Grill to indirect cooking at 400°F

2. Pour 1/2 cup of evaporated milk in a saucepan and allow to cook over low heat until its warm, add condensed milk and yeast in a bowl and leave for 5 minutes.

3. Mix the flour with two cups of evaporated milk, butter, salt, and the yeast in a bowl.

4. Mix all ingredient in a bowl until dough forms ball, if the dough proves sticky add more flour

5. Place dough in an oiled bowl, cover with plastic wrap and put in a warm place for 2-1/2 hours for it to double in size

6. Mix egg and water in a bowl, put doubled dough on a work surface and flatten with palm, knead and divide the dough then roll it and brush with oil

7. Spread 1/4 cup of tapenade over dough plus 1/2 cup of pepper, sprinkle with a cup of cheese, roll up and allow to double for 45 minutes

8. Brush with mixed egg and bake for 45 minutes remove from oven and rest it for 10 minutes before slicing.

Pita Bread

Prep time: 1 hour | Cook time: 2 hours | Serves: 12

Ingredients:

- 1/2 cup of warm water
- 2 tsp of honey
- 1-1/2 tsp of yeast
- 2 Tbsp of extra virgin oil
- 2 tsp of kosher salt
- 1-1/2 cup of wheat flour
- 2 cups plus 1/2 cup of all-purpose flour

Directions:

1. Set Grill to direct cooking at 400^0F
2. Pour a cup of water plus honey into Dutch oven, stir until honey dissolves, sprinkle yeast over water, then leave for about 10 minutes
3. Put olive oil and salt with whole wheat flour with 2 cups of all-purpose flour in a bowl add the yeast mixture and mix for 3 minutes with mixer until dough forms ball.
4. Add flour until dough is no stickier, knead for about 8 minutes, then place dough on the work surface and mold into a ball in an oiled bowl, cover bowl, and set aside for an hour.
5. Form dough into an 18-inch log and cut into 12 pieces, form each piece into ball and place on pan, cover and place aside for about 12 minutes.
6. Place ball on the work surface and roll into disk, place disk in preheated oven bake for about 4 minutes, then turn over and bake for 2 hours until it turns golden brown.

Naan Bread

Prep time: 2 hours | Cook time: 10 minutes | Serves: 8

Ingredients:

- 3 cups of bread flour
- 1 tsp of yeast
- 1 tsp of table salt
- 2 Tbsp of sunflower oil
- 1 tsp of honey
- 3/4 cup of warm water
- 4 Tbsp of plain low-fat yogurt.

Directions:

1. Set Grill to direct cooking at 400^0F
2. Place yeast, flour in a bowl and add salt, use wooden spoon stir well until its mixed
3. Add the sunflower oil, water, yogurt, honey mix gently until dough forms, place dough on the work surface, form dough into a ball
4. Place into oiled bowl cover dough and let it rise for about 2 hours
5. Turn dough unto work surface and cut in 8 equal pieces, roll each piece into a ball, using rolling pin roll ball into 1/2 inch thick disk
6. Place the disk in the oven and bake for about 5 minutes until its golden brown.

Buttermilk Biscuit

Prep time: 30 minutes | Cook time: 30 minutes | Serves: 12

Ingredients:

- 1-1/2 cup of cake flour
- 1 cup of all-purpose flour
- 4 tsp of baking powder
- 1/2 tsp of baking soda
- 1 Tbsp of granulated sugar
- 1 Tbsp of salt
- 8 Tbsp of unsalted butter, cubed
- 1/2 cup of solid vegetable shortening

- 1-1/4 cups of buttermilk, cold

Directions:

1. Set the Grill to indirect cooking at 400°F
2. Sift cake flour, sugar, baking soda and powder, all-purpose flour, and salt together in a large bowl, add butter and shortening
3. With the use of fork work butter and shortening into flour until the butter is pea-sized. With fork stir buttermilk into flour until dough forms ball
4. Turn dough on the work surface with the use of rolling pin roll dough into a 1-inch thick rectangle, dust with flour to prevent sticking
5. Fold the dough into thirds, roll again into 1-inch thick rectangle, use the 3-inch diameter cookie cutter to cut dough into 10 biscuits.
6. Place biscuit side by side in the baking dish, bake for about 22 minutes until golden brown.

Spicy Spanish Frittata with Chorizo

Prep time: 30minutes | Cook time: 40minutes | serves: 8

Ingredients:

- 10 large eggs, beaten
- 1/2 cup of heavy cream
- 1/2 tsp of kosher salt
- 1/4 tsp of freshly grounded black pepper
- 1 cup of diced, grilled chorizo
- 1/4 cup of chopped grilled scallions
- 34 cup of shredded manchego cheese
- 1/4 cup of chopped pimientos
- 1/4 cup of fresh green peas
- 1/4 tsp of smoked Spanish paprika

Directions:

1. Set the Grill to indirect cooking at 400°F
2. Mix the egg, salt, cream, and pepper in a bowl. Pour the mixture into an oiled baking dish
3. Add the egg mixture, chorizo, scallions, cheese, pimientos, and peas sprinkled with paprika one at a time
4. Place dish in the oven and bake for about 35 minutes
5. Rest frittata for about 10 minutes before serving.

Stone Ground Grits and Sausage Casserole

Prep time: 15minutes | Cook time: 1 hour | serves: 8

Ingredients:

- 5 cups of water
- 2-1/2 cups of white stone-ground grits
- 1 cup of heavy cream
- 2 cups plus 2 cups shredded white cheddar cheese
- 8 Tbsp of unsalted butter, cubed
- 1 pound of pork sausage, grilled and chopped
- 1/2 cup of sliced fresh chives
- 2 tsp of kosher salt
- 1/2 tsp of freshly ground black pepper
- 1 cup of panko (Japanese bread crumbs)

Directions:

1. Set the Grill to indirect cooking at 400°F
2. Boil water in a large pot, add grits and simmer for about 35minutes stir occasionally to prevent sticking until water is absorbed
3. Grits from the heat add cream, add 2 cups of cheese, butter, sausage chives, salt and pepper
4. Mix until the cheese is melted, pour grits into an oiled baking dish with the use of

spatula spread evenly

5. Top with the 2 cups of cheese remaining sprinkle panko on cheese
6. Place dish in the oven and bake for 30 minutes.

Southwestern Cornbread

Prep time: 30 minutes | Cook time: 30 minutes | Serves: 8

Ingredients:

- 2 cups of cornmeal
- 1 cup of all-purpose flour
- 2 tsp of baking powder
- 2 tsp of table salt
- 2 cups of buttermilk
- 2 large eggs, beaten
- 1/2 cup of sour cream
- 4 Tbsp of unsalted butter, melted
- 1 cup of roasted yellow corn kernels
- 3/4 cup diced red bell pepper
- 2 jalapenos, seeded and chopped

Direction:

1. Set the Grill to indirect cooking at 400^{0}F
2. Mix cornmeal, flour, baking powder, and salt in a bowl, add buttermilk, eggs, sour cream, butter, corn, bell pepper, and jalapenos, with the use of spatula mix all the ingredients together
3. Pour mixture into a baking dish, spread evenly with spatula place in the oven
4. Bake for about 25 minutes

Apple Pancake

Prep time: 40 minutes | Cook time: 20 minutes | serves: 8

Ingredients:

- 2 Tbsp of granulated sugar
- 1/4 tsp table salt
- 1/2 tsp ground cinnamon

- 2 large eggs, whisked
- 1/4 tsp of kosher salt
- Confectioners sugar for dusting
- 1/2 tsp of vanilla extract
- 1/4 tsp ground nutmeg
- 2 granny smith apples, cored, peeled and chopped
- 1 Tbsp of lemon zest
- 1/2 cup of brown sugar
- 1/2 cup of all-purpose flour
- 4 Tbsp of unsalted butter
- 1 cup of heavy cream
- 2 Tbsp of freshly squeezed lemon

Directions:

1. Set the Grill to direct cooking at 400^{0}F
2. Preheat the pie plate for about 30 minutes, mix flour, sugar, table salt, eggs, cream, and vanilla in a bowl, mix well
3. Place apple slice in a bowl, add cinnamon, nutmeg, lemon zest, and kosher salt
4. Place butter in the hot pie plate to melt, pour apple mixture into the butter, saute for about 10 minutes until the apples become tender
5. Add lemon juice with a sprinkle of brown sugar, pour batter evenly on top of apple mixture
6. Remove pie plate from heat place in oven and allow to bake for about 12 minutes until butter is firm
7. Move to the baking dish and allow to cool, dust with confectioners' sugar and serve.

Tropical Breakfast Muffins

Prep time: 30minutes | Cook time: 20minutes | serves: 8

Ingredients:

- 2 cups of all-purpose flour

- 1 tsp of baking powder
- 1 tsp of baking soda
- 1/2 tsp of table salt
- 1/2 cup of granulated sugar
- 8 Tbsp of unsalted butter, melted
- 1/2 cup half and half
- 3 large eggs
- 1 Tbsp of coconut extract
- 2 cups of diced fresh pineapple
- 1-1/2 cup of shredded sweetened coconut
- 1 cup of crushed macadamia nuts
- 8 oz. white chocolate chunks

Directions:

1. Set the Grill at 400°F
2. Mix flour, baking soda, baking powder, salt, and sugar in a bowl. Add butter, eggs, and coconut extract to the mixture, then stir with a spatula.
3. Fold pineapple, coconut, macadamia, nuts, and white chocolate into the batter, fill prepared muffin pan cup three-quarter full using a spoon
4. Place filled pan in the oven and allow to bake for 20 minutes
5. Remove the muffin and serve.

Banana Foster

Prep time: 10minutes | Cook time: 10minutes | serves: 8

Ingredients:

- 8 Tbsp of unsalted butter
- 1/2 cup of firmly packed brown sugar
- 1/2 cup of granulated sugar
- 1/2 tsp of ground cinnamon
- 4 bananas, peeled and sliced lengthwise
- 1/4 cup of banana liqueur
- 1/2 cup of dark rum
- pint vanilla ice cream

Directions:

1. Set Grill at 400°F
2. Mix butter, brown sugar, granulated sugar, and cinnamon in a dutch oven. Cook for about four minutes, continually whisking until smooth. Add banana, cut side down and cook for about 3 minutes until banana is coated in sugar mixture, add rum and banana liqueur to it
3. Light the liqueur and rum, cook until flames burn off
4. Portion the ice cream Into a bowl, then spoon the banana sauce over the top and serve.

Chocolate Pecan Bourbon Pie

Prep time: 2 hours 30 minutes | Cook time: 50 minutes | Serves: 8

Ingredients:

- 1 pie shell, 9 inches
- 5 Tbsp of unsalted butter, melted
- 1 cup of firmly packed brown sugar
- 3 large eggs, beaten
- 1/4 cup of bourbon
- 1 cup semisweet chocolate chips
- 2 Tbsp of all-purpose flour
- 1 cup of chopped pecans
- 1 cup of dark corn syrup

WHIPPED CREAM

- 1/2 tsp of vanilla extract
- 1/2 cup of confectioners' sugar
- 1 cup of heavy cream

Directions:

1. Set Grill at 400°F
2. Mix eggs, butter, corn syrup, brown sugar, bourbon, and flour in a bowl using a wooden spoon
3. Add chocolate and pecans then blend well, pour fillings into pie shell
4. Place pie plate in the oven and bake for about 45 minutes, remove pie to cool

then refrigerate

5. Make whip cream with a whisker or electric mixer, beat cream, confectioner sugar and vanilla for about 5 minutes
6. Garnish with whip cream and serve sliced pie.

Red Chile and Lime Shortbread Cookies

Prep time: 30 minutes | Cook time: 20 minutes | Serves: 12

Ingredients:

- 8 Tbsp of unsalted butter
- 1/4 cup of granulated sugar
- 1/2 tsp of table salt
- 2 tsp of lime zest
- 1 tsp of red Chile rub
- 1 cup plus 2 Tbsp of all-purpose flour

Directions:

1. Set the Grill at 400^{0}F
2. Mix butter, sugar, salt, lime zest, and red Chile rub in a large bowl using an electric mixer until butter is creamed but not completely smooth
3. Add flour to the mixture and knead until it forms a dough. Transfer dough to a lightly floured work surface, roll with a rolling pin into 1/4 inch thick, then place the dough in a cake pan. Spread evenly with fingers and press dough into the edges of the pan
4. Cut dough into about 12 equal wedges; do not cut all through the dough. Place cake pan in oven and bake for about 8 minutes until light brown
5. Serve when cool.

Chapter 11: Searing Recipe

Reverse-Seared Halibut

Prep and Cooking time: 50 mins | Serves: 4

Ingredients To Use:

- halibut fillet (skin removed)
- 1 tsp of salt
- 1 tsp grounded black pepper
- 1 tsp of dried basil
- 1 tbsp lemon juice
- Pinch of chopped parsley
- tbsps olive oil.

Step-by-Step Directions:

1. Preheat the Smoker-grill for direct cooking at 300^0 F.
2. In a large bowl, add the fillets, salt, basil, olive oil, salt, pepper, and lemon juice. Cover and refrigerate for 30 minutes.
3. Grill the halibut for 30 minutes, then set aside.
4. Increase the temperature to 450^0 F and allow the temperature of the grill to rise.
5. Sear halibut for 3 minutes per side. Remove and garnish with parsley.

Seared Venison Chops with Marsala

Prep Time and Cooking time: 1 hour 10 minutes | Serves: 6

Ingredients To Use:

- 1 cup marsala wine
- Venison chops
- 3 Tbsp unsalted butter
- 2 Tbsp olive oil
- 1 cup of beef stock
- 1 tsp fresh sage, finely chopped
- 1 cup of beef stock
- Salt and pepper to taste
- peeled shallot

Step-by-Step Directions:

1. Set the Smoker-grill to direct cooking at 300^0 F
2. Rinse the venison and pat dry with a paper towel. Season with salt and pepper.
3. Grill both sides of venison for 30 minutes, then set aside and increase the temperature of the grill to *High.*
4. Place a skillet over cooking grates, add oil and sear venison for 4 minutes per side. Set aside.
5. Place a small pot over cooking grates, melt 1 tbsp of butter and sauté the shallot for 5 minutes, or until they are brown.
6. Add the stock, marsala, and sage and allow it to simmer for 15-20 minutes. Add the remaining butter, season with salt and pepper.
7. Serve with the venison.

Reverse Sear Tri-Tip

Prep Time: 10 minutes | Cook Time: 1 hour | Serves: 6

Ingredients:

- 2lb Tri-Tip
- Olive Oil
- Barbeque Sauce (recipe in chapter 9)

Directions:

1. Preheat your Grill to 300°F
2. Rub the barbeque sauce and olive oil on the tri-tip. Allow to marinate for about 3

minutes.

3. Place the tri-tip on a drip pan in the Grill and cook indirect for about 45 minutes or until internal temperature records 130°F
4. Place the tri-tip in a cast iron pan to sear for 2 minutes per side.
5. Serve with Fennel Salsa

Reverse-Seared Ribeye

Prep Time: 20 minutes | Cook Time: 1 hour | Serves: 6

Ingredients:

- 5lb whole boneless ribeye, cut into 2-inch thick steaks
- 1/4 cup of salt
- 1/4 cup pepper
- 1/4 cup finely chopped tarragon,
- 1/4 cup finely chopped thyme
- 1/4 cup finely chopped parsley
- 1lb salted butter, at room temperature

Directions:

1. Install Plate Setter for indirect cooking at temperature of 275°F.
2. Mix the salt and pepper to create a rub, then apply it on the steaks.
3. Combine the herbs and butter to make a compound seasoning—massage 1 Tbsp of compound seasoning on each of the steaks. Reserve the rest of the seasoning.
4. Arrange the steaks on the cast iron and roast for 45 minutes or until internal temperature records 115°F. Set the steaks aside and remove the Plate Setter for direct cooking.
5. Sear steaks for 2 minutes per side.
6. Allow to cool for 10 minutes before serving. Top steaks with 1 Tbsp of reserved compound seasoning

Reverse-Seared Bacon Weave Pork Tenderloin

Prep Time: 10 minutes | Cook Time: 1 hour | Serves: 5

Ingredients:

- 1lb packaged bacon
- 1 pork tenderloin
- 6 Tbsp Black Peppercorn Rub (recipe in Chapter 9)

Directions:

1. Install Plate Setter for indirect cooking at 400°F
2. Weave the bacon.
3. Sprinkle 4 Tbsp of black peppercorn rub over the tenderloin, then mix well. Wrap the tenderloin with the bacon weaves and secure with skewers. Rub the rest of the black peppercorn rub over the wrapped pork loin.
4. Arrange the tenderloin over the Rib & Roast Rack, then roast for 20 minutes or until an internal temperature of 145°F is measured.
5. Remove the Plate Setter for direct cooking at 600°F. Then sear wrapped pork loin for 2 minutes per side.

Presa Iberico

Prep Time: 30 minutes | Cook Time: 30 minutes | Serves: 3

Ingredients:

- 16 ounces of Presa Iberico
- 1/2 tsp salt
- 4 Tbsp Alabama White BBQ Sauce (recipe in chapter 9)

Directions:

1. Positon the Plate Setter for indirect grilling at 250°F.

2. Trim off any excess fat on the Presa Iberico, then rub the Alabama White BBQ Sauce all over it.
3. Place the meat on the cast iron and roast for 30 minutes or until internal temperature records 136°F.
4. Set the meat aside and remove the Plate Setter for direct cooking at 600°F.
5. Sear meat for 2 minutes per side.
6. Allow to cool before serving.

Reverse-Seared Pork Steaks

Prep Time: 5 minutes | Cook Time: 1 hour | Serves: 2

Ingredients:
- Two pork steaks, 1-1/2 inches thick
- 4 tsp of red chile pepper rub
- Korean BBQ sauce
- Salt and black pepper, to taste

Directions:
1. Install Plate Setter for indirect grilling at 225°F
2. Coat the steaks with red chile pepper rub, salt, and black pepper.
3. Place steaks on the cast iron and roast/smoke for 30 minutes or until internal temperature measures 160°F.
4. Set the meat aside and remove the Plate Setter for direct cooking at to 600°F
5. Sear meat for 2 minutes per side.
6. Install Plate Setter for indirect cooking at 225°F.
7. Coat the meat with the Korean Barbeque Sauce, then return to the cast iron grill.
8. Keep coating the steaks periodically with the barbeque sauce over the next 15 minutes.
9. Allow to cool before serving.

Cranberry-Marinated Rack of

Lamb

Prep Time: 5 minutes | Cook Time: 4 hours | Serves: 2

Ingredients:
- 1 cup of pomegranate juice
- 1 cup of red wine
- 1/2 cup of cranberries
- 1 fresh rosemary sprig
- 2 Tbsp olive oil
- 2 Australian lamb racks, frenched
- Salt and ground pepper, to taste

Directions:
1. Place lamb racks in a medium bowl. Add red wine, cranberries, pomegranate juice, and rosemary. Marinate for 3 hours (for a vibrant taste allow to soak overnight).
2. Install Plate Setter for indirect grilling at 400°F.
3. Remove lamb racks from marinade and pat with a towel to remove excess juice. Bring marinade to a boil in a saucepan, then reduce heat and allow to simmer until it is reduced to a thin glaze. Throw away the rosemary sprig.
4. Add oil to the Cast Iron Dutch Oven then sear both sides of the lamb until they brown.
5. Remove Dutch Oven from Grill, then arrange the lamb racks on the grid and grill 10 minutes for medium-rare.
6. Allow to cool before cutting into chops and serving.

Cast Iron Seared T-Bone Steak

Prep Time: 10 minutes | Cook Time: 1 hour | Serves: 5

Ingredients:
- 1 bone-in T-bone steak, 2-inch thick
- Salt and black pepper, to taste

- 1/4 cup grapeseed oil
- 3 Tbsp unsalted butter
- 6 thyme sprigs
- 1 large shallot, thinly sliced

Directions:

1. Pat steak dry with a paper towel. Season both sides with salt and black pepper and allow to marinate for 30 minutes at room temperature.
2. Remove the Plate Setter for direct cooking at 550°F.
3. Add Grill's Cast Iron Dutch Oven to the cooking grid. Pour oil into Dutch Oven and heat until it sizzles, then add the steak. Cook, flipping once until a golden-brown crust develops. This will take about 3 minutes.
4. Add the herbs, butter, and shallots to the Dutch Oven and continue cooking, flipping the steak periodically and basting butter on light spots.
5. Continue basting and searing until a thermometer inserted into the thickest part of the meat measures 120-125°F for medium-rare. This will take about 6 to q0 minutes.
6. Allow to rest on a large platter for 10 minutes before carving. Enjoy!

Chapter 12: Marinade, Rub and Sauce

Texas-Style Brisket Rub

Prep Time and Cooking time: 15 minutes | Serves: 1

Ingredients To Use:

- 2 tsp Sugar
- 2 Tbsp Kosher salt
- 2 tsp Chilli powder
- 2 Tbsp Black pepper
- Tbsp Cayenne pepper
- Tbsp Powdered garlic
- tsp Grounded cumin
- 2 Tbsp Powdered onion
- 1/4 cup paprika, smoked

Step-by-Step Directions:

1. Mix all the ingredients in a small bowl until it is well blended.
2. Transfer to an airtight jar or container. Store in a cool place.

Pork Dry Rub

Prep Time and Cooking time: 15 minutes | Serves: 1 cup

Ingredients To Use:

- Tbsp Kosher salt
- 2 Tbsp Powered onions
- Tbsp Cayenne pepper
- 1tsp Dried mustard
- 1/4 cup brown sugar
- Tbsp Powdered garlic
- Tbsp Powdered chili pepper
- 1/4 cup smoked paprika
- 2 Tbsp Black pepper

Step-by-Step Directions:

1. Combine all the ingredients in a small bowl.
2. Transfer to an airtight jar or container.
3. Keep stored in a cool, dry place.

Texas Barbeque Rub

Prep Time and Cooking time: 15 minutes | Serves: 1/2 cup

Ingredients To Use:

- 1 tsp Sugar
- Tbsp Seasoned salt
- Tbsp Black pepper
- tsp Chilli powder
- Tbsp Powdered onions
- Tbsp Smoked paprika
- 1 tsp Sugar
- Tbsp Powdered garlic

Step-by-Step Directions:

1. Pour all the ingredients into a small bowl and mix thoroughly.
2. Keep stored in an airtight jar or container.

Barbeque Sauce

This is a classic sauce with the right amount of sweetness and spice. If you are interested in a simple sauce for your barbecue, this is perfect.

Prep Time and Cooking time: 15 minutes | Serves: 2 cups

Ingredients To Use:

- 1/4 cup of water
- 1/4 cup red wine vinegar
- Tbsp Worcestershire sauce
- 1 tsp Paprika
- 1 tsp Salt

- Tbsp Dried mustard
- 1 tsp black pepper
- 1 cup ketchup
- 1 cup brown sugar

Step-by-Step Directions:

1. Pour all the ingredients into a food processor, one after the other.
2. Process until they are evenly mixed.
3. Transfer sauce to a close lid jar. Store in the refridgerator.

Steak Sauce

Prep Time and Cooking time: 25 minutes | Serves: 1/2 cup

Ingredients To Use:

- Tbsp Malt vinegar
- 1/2 tsp Salt
- 1/2 tsp black pepper
- Tbsp Tomato sauce
- 2 Tbsp brown sugar
- 1 tsp hot pepper sauce
- 2 Tbsp Worcestershire sauce
- 2 Tbsp Raspberry jam.

Step-by-Step Directions:

1. Preheat your grill for indirect cooking at 150°F
2. Place a saucepan over grates, add all your ingredients, and allow to boil.
3. Reduce the temperature to *Smoke* and allow the sauce to simmer for 10 minutes or until sauce is thick.

Bourbon Whiskey Sauce

Prep Time and Cooking time: 45 minutes | Serves: 3 cup

Ingredients To Use:

- cups ketchup
- 1/4 cup Worcestershire sauce
- 3/4 cup bourbon whiskey

- 1/3 cup apple cider vinegar
- 1/2 onions, minced
- 1/4 cup of tomato paste
- cloves of garlic, minced
- 1/2 tsp Black pepper
- 1/2 cup brown sugar
- 1/2 Tbsp Salt
- Hot pepper sauce to taste
- Tbsp Liquid smoke flavoring

Step-by-Step Directions:

1. Preheat your grill for indirect cooking at 150°F
2. Place a saucepan over grates, then add the whiskey, garlic, and onions.
3. Simmer until the onion is translucent. Then add the other ingredients and adjust the temperature to *Smoke*. Simmer for 20 minutes. For a smooth sauce, sieve.

Chicken Marinade

Prep Time and Cooking time: 35 minutes | Serves: 3 cups

Ingredients To Use:

- halved chicken breast (bone and skin removed)
- Tbsp Spicy brown mustard
- 2/3 cup of soy sauce
- tsp Powdered garlic
- 2 Tbsp Liquid smoke flavoring
- 2/3 cup extra virgin olive oil
- 2/3 cup lemon juice
- 2 tsp Black pepper

Step-by-Step Directions:

1. Mix all the ingredients in a large bowl.
2. Pour the chicken into the bowl and allow it to marinate for about 3-4hours in the refrigerator. Remove the chicken, then smoke, grill, or roast the chicken.

Nutritional value per serving:

Calories: 507kcal, Carbs:46.6g Fat: 41.8g, Protein: 28g

Carne Asada Marinade

Prep Time and Cooking time: 2hours | Serves: 5 cups

Ingredients To Use:

- cloves garlic, chopped
- tsp Lemon juice
- 1/2 cup extra virgin olive oil
- 1/2 tsp Salt
- 1/2 tsp Pepper

Step-by-Step Directions:

1. Mix all your ingredients in a bowl.
2. Pour the beef into the bowl and allow to marinate for 2-3hours before grilling.

Grapefruit Juice Marinade

Prep Time and Cooking time: 1hours 10 minutes | Serves: 3 cups

Ingredients To Use:

- 1/2 reduced-sodium soy sauce
- cups grapefruit juice, unsweetened
- 1-1/2 lb. Chicken, bone and skin removed
- 1/4 brown sugar

Step-by-Step Directions:

1. Thoroughly mix all your ingredients in a large bowl.
2. Add the chicken and allow it to marinate for 2-3 hours before grilling.

Steak Marinade

Prep Time and Cooking time: 15 minutes | Serves: 2cups

Ingredients To Use:

- Tbsp Worcestershire sauce
- Tbsp Red wine vinegar
- 1/2 cup barbeque sauce
- Tbsp soy sauce
- 1/4 cup steak sauce
- 1 clove garlic (minced)
- 1 tsp Mustard
- Pepper and salt to taste

Step-by-Step Directions:

1. Pour all the ingredients in a bowl and mix thoroughly.
2. Use immediately or keep refrigerated.

Smoked Tomato Cream Sauce

Prep time: 15 minutes, Cook time: 1 hour 20 minutes; Serves 1

Ingredients

- 1 lb beefsteak tomatoes, fresh and quartered
- 1-1/2 tbsp olive oil
- Black pepper, freshly ground
- Salt, kosher
- 1/2 cup yellow onions, chopped
- 1 tbsp tomato paste
- 2 tbsp minced garlic
- Pinch cayenne
- 1/2 cup chicken stock
- 1/2 cup heavy cream

Preparation Method

1. Prepare your smoker using directions from the manufacturer.
2. Toss tomatoes and 1 tbsp oil in a bowl, mixing, then season with pepper and salt.
3. Smoke the tomatoes placed on a smoker rack for about 30 minutes. Remove and set aside reserving tomato juices.
4. Heat 1/2 tbsp oil in a saucepan over high-medium heat.
5. Add onion and cook for about 3-4 minutes. Add tomato paste and garlic then cook for an additional 1 minute.
6. Add smoked tomatoes, cayenne, tomato

juices, pepper, and salt then cook for about 3-4 minutes. Stir often.

7. Add chicken stock and boil for about 25-30 minutes under a gentle simmer. Stir often.

8. Place the mixture in a blender and puree until smooth. Now squeeze the mixture through a sieve, fine-mesh, to discard solids and release the juices,

9. Transfer the sauce in a saucepan, small, and add the cream.

10. Simmer for close to 6 minutes over low-medium heat until thickened slightly. Season with pepper and salt.

11. Serve warm with risotto cakes.

Smoked Mushroom Sauce

Prep time: 30 minutes, Cook time: 1 hour; serves 4

Ingredients

- 1-quart chef mix mushrooms
- 2 tbsp canola oil
- 1/4 cup julienned shallots
- 2 tbsp chopped garlic
- Salt and pepper to taste
- 1/4 cup alfasi cabernet sauvignon
- 1 cup beef stock
- 2 tbsp margarine

Preparation Method

1. Crumple four foil sheets into balls. Puncture multiple places in the foil pan then place mushrooms in the foil pan. Smoke in a Grill for about 30 minutes. Remove and cool.

2. Heat canola oil in a pan, sauté, add shallots and sauté until translucent.

3. Add mushrooms and cook until supple and rendered down.

4. Add garlic and season with pepper and salt. Cook until fragrant.

5. Add beef stock and wine then cook for about 6-8 minutes over low heat. Adjust seasoning.

6. Add margarine and stir until sauce is thickened and a nice sheen.

7. Serve and enjoy!

Smoked Cranberry Sauce

Prep time: 10 minutes, Cook time: 1 hour; Serves 2

Ingredients

- 12 oz bag cranberries
- 2 chunks ginger, quartered
- 1 cup apple cider
- 1 tbsp honey whiskey
- 5.5 oz fruit juice
- 1/8 tbsp ground cloves
- 1/8 tbsp cinnamon
- 1/2 orange zest
- 1/2 orange
- 1 tbsp maple syrup
- 1 apple, diced and peeled
- 1/2 cup sugar
- 1/2 brown sugar

Preparation Method

1. Preheat your Grill to 375°F.

2. Place cranberries in a pan then add all other ingredients.

3. Place the pan on the grill and cook for about 1 hour until cooked through.

4. Remove ginger pieces and squeeze juices from the orange into tthe sauce.

5. Serve and enjoy!

Smoked sriracha sauce

Prep time: 10 minutes, Cook time: 1 hour; serves 2

Ingredients

- 1 lb Fresno chiles, stems pulled off and

seeds removed
- 1/2 cup rice vinegar
- 1/2 cup red wine vinegar
- 1 carrot, medium and cut into rounds, 1/4 inch
- 1-1/2 tbsp sugar, dark-brown
- 4 garlic cloves, peeled
- 1 tbsp olive oil
- 1 tbsp kosher salt
- 1/2 cup water

Preparation Method

1. Smoke chiles in a smoker for about 15 minutes.
2. Bring to boil both vinegars then add carrots, sugar, and garlic. Simmer for about 15 minutes while covered. Cool for 30 minutes.
3. Place the chiles, olive oil, vinegar-vegetable mixture, salt, and 1/4 cup water into a blender.
4. Blend for about 1-2 minutes on high. Add remaining water and blend again. You can add another 1/4 cup water if you want your sauce thinner.
5. Pour the sauce into jars and place in a refrigerator.
6. Serve.

Smoked soy sauce

Prep time: 15 minutes, Cook time: 1 hour; Serves 1

Ingredients

- 100ml soy sauce
- Bradley flavor bisquettes cherry

Preparation Method

1. Put soy sauce in a heat-resistant bowl, large-mouth.
2. Smoke in a smoker at 158-176°F for about 1 hour. Stir a few times.
3. Remove and cool then put in a bottle.

Let sit for one day.
4. Serve and enjoy!

Smoked Garlic Sauce

Prep time: 5 minutes, Cook time: 30 minutes; Serves 2

Ingredients

- 3 whole garlic heads
- 1/2 cup mayonnaise
- 1/4 cup sour cream
- 2 tbsp lemon juice
- 2 tbsp cider vinegar
- Salt to taste

Preparation Method

1. Cut the garlic heads off then place in a microwave-safe bowl, add 2 tbsp water and cover. Microwave for about 5-6 minutes on medium.
2. Heat your grill on medium.
3. Place the garlic heads in a shallow 'boat' foil and smoke for about 20-25 minutes until soft.
4. Transfer the garlic heads into a blender. Process for a few minutes until smooth.
5. Add remaining ingredients and process until everything is combined.
6. Enjoy!

Smoked Cherry BBQ Sauce

Prep time: 20 minutes, Cook time: 1 hour; Serves 2

Ingredients

- 2 lb dark sweet cherries, pitted
- 1 large chopped onion
- 1/2 tbsp red pepper flakes, crushed
- 1 tbsp kosher salt or to taste
- 1/2 tbsp ginger, ground
- 1/2 tbsp black pepper
- 1/2 tbsp cumin

- 1/2 tbsp cayenne pepper
- 1 tbsp onion powder
- 1 tbsp garlic powder
- 1 tbsp smoked paprika
- 2 chopped garlic cloves
- 1/2 cup pinot noir
- 2 tbsp yellow mustard
- 1-1/2 cups ketchup
- 2 tbsp balsamic vinegar
- 1/3 cup apple cider vinegar
1. 2 tbsp dark soy sauce

Red Chile Spice Rub

Prep time: 5 minutes| Cook time: 5 minutes| Yields: 3/4 cup

Ingredients:

- 4 dried Cascabel chiles
- 4 dried Ancho chiles
- 4 dried Mexico chiles
- 1/2 cup cumin seeds
- 1 Tbsp Coriander seeds
- 1 tsp garlic powder
- 1 Tbsp kosher salt

Directions:

1. Preheat a small Dutch Oven and roast the dried chiles, cumin, and coriander seeds on the cooking grid until very fragrant. It will take about 5 minutes. Transfer roasted spice to a bowl, and then stir in garlic powder and kosher salt.
2. Grind the spices with a spice grinder or food processor until the mixture is fine and smooth.
3. Store in an airtight container for up to 3 months.

Dry Chicken Rub

Prep time: 5 minutes| Cook time: - minutes| Yields: 1/4 cup

Ingredients:

- 1 Tbsp salt
- 2 Tsp garlic powder
- 1 Tsp paprika
- 1 Tsp ground mustard
- 1 Tsp ground black pepper
- 1 Tsp garlic powder
- Tsp onion powder, ground oregano, and brown sugar
- Tbsp dried Italian herb
- 1/2 Tsp cayenne pepper

Directions:

1. Using a spatula, mix all ingredients in a small bowl. Store in an airtight container at room temperature.

Barbecue Rub

Prep time: 5 minutes| Cook time: - minutes| Yields: 1 cup

Ingredients:

- 1/4 cup brown sugar, tightly packed
- 1/4 cup sweet paprika
- 2 Tsp kosher salt
- 1/4 cup ground cumin
- 1Tsp ground chili pepper
- 4 Tbsp cayenne pepper
- 1 Tbsp onion powder
- 1/4 cup dry mustard

Directions:

1. Mix all of the ingredients in a bowl until an excellent consistency is obtained.
2. Pour into an airtight container, then seal. Store away from moisture.

Black Peppercorn Rub

Prep time: 6 minutes| Cook time: - minutes| Yields: 1/4 cup

Ingredients:

- 1 tsp Paprika
- 1 Tbsp black peppercorn

- 1 Tbsp fresh oregano leaves
- 1 Tbsp clove garlic, minced
- 1 tsp onion powder
- 1/2 tsp ground thyme
- 1/4 tsp salt

Directions:

1. Combine all ingredients in a food processor and pulse until finely ground.

Korean BBQ Sauce

This Korean recipe is a total taste bud buster that's quick and easy-to-make. It is sticky and also has a sweet, savory, and spicy taste.
Prep time: 5 minutes| Cook time: 10 minutes| Yields: 2 cups

Ingredients:

- 1 cup Tamari
- 3/4 cup brown sugar
- 4 garlic clove, minced
- 1 thumb ginger, grated
- 1 Tbsp rice wine vinegar
- 2 Tsp cayenne pepper
- 1 Tsp chili pepper
- 2 Tsp maple syrup
- 2 Tsp corn starch
- 1 Tbsp water

Directions:

1. Preheat a saucepan. Stir in Tamari, brown sugar, clove, ginger, rice wine vinegar, cayenne pepper, chili pepper, and maple syrup. Bring to boil under medium-high heat.
2. Mix cornstarch and water in a bowl, then pour the dissolved mixture into the spice mixture and stir cook until the mixture thickens.
3. Remove from heat and allow to cool. Place sauce in an airtight container and store in the refrigerator fridge for up to two weeks.

Holy Smoke Basting Sauce

Prep time: 5 minutes| Cook time: 10 minutes| Yields: 2 cups

Ingredients:

- 4 cups apple cider vinegar
- 1 cup Worcestershire sauce
- 1 Tbsp ground black pepper
- 3/4 cup lemon juice
- A pinch of cardamom

Directions

1. Add all ingredients into a medium-size saucepan.
2. Boil for 10 minutes over medium-high heat.
3. Remove from heat and use sauce to baste smoking or grilling meat.

Texas Hillbilly Mop Sauce

Prep time: 5 minutes| Cook time: 10 minutes| Serves: 1-1/2 cup

Ingredients:

- 2 cups apple cider vinegar
- 1/2 cup of water
- 1 cup olive oil
- 1 Tbsp garlic, minced
- 1 tbsp chilli powder
- 3/4 cup Worcestershire sauce
- 1 Tbsp paprika
- A handful of bay leaves
- 2 Tbsp hot sauce
- 1/2 cup squeezed lemon juice

Directions:

1. Transfer all ingredients into a pot on a cooking grid and bring to a boil under medium-high heat. Afterward, bring to simmer for 10 minutes under medium-low heat.
2. Turn off heat and cool sauce slightly.

3. Use mop sauce over meat while cooking.

Alabama White BBQ Sauce

Prep time: 10 minutes| Cook time: 0 minute|
Serves: 2 cups

Ingredients:

- 2 cups mayonnaise
- 1 Tbsp ground black pepper
- 1/2 cup vinegar
- 1 tsp kosher salt
- 1 tsp chilli pepper
- 1 tbsp garlic, minced
- 2 Tbsp lemon juice
- 1 Tbsp ground mustard
- 1 Tsp garlic powder

Directions:

1. Pour apple cider, vinegar, mayonnaise, and lemon juice in a bowl, and then whisk until a smooth, creamy consistency is obtained.
2. Add salt, garlic, ginger, garlic, mustard, chili pepper, and black pepper. Cover mixture and place in a refrigerator for 30 min before using.

Sun-Dried Tomato Pesto Sauce

Prep time: 15 minutes| Cook time: - minute|
Serves: 2 cups

Ingredients:

- 1 cup sun-dried tomatoes in oil
- 3 cloves garlic, minced
- 2 Tbsp balsamic vinegar
- 1/2 Tsp ground chili pepper
- 1/3 cup roasted almonds
- 1/2 cup grated parmesan cheese
- 1/4 cup olive oil
- 1/2 cup parsley

Directions:

1. Process tomatoes in a food processor until finely chopped.
2. Slowly add almonds, chili pepper, garlic, cheese, parsley, cheese, vinegar, and olive oil while the food processor is running. Blend until smooth.
3. Transfer sauce in an airtight container and store for up to one week in a refrigerator.

KC Classic Barbeque Sauce

Prep time: 5 minutes| Cook time: 10 minutes|
Yields: 4 cups

Ingredients:

- 1 tsp ground black pepper
- 1/2 cup red wine vinegar
- 1/4 cup squeezed lemon juice
- 2 cups ketchup
- 1/4 cup dark molasses
- 1/2 cup maple syrup
- 1/2 Tsp garlic powder
- 1/2 Tsp onion powder
- 1 cup brown sugar, tightly packed
- 1/2 cup apple cider vinegar
- 1 tsp kosher salt
- 1 tsp ground pepper
- 1/2cup yellow mustard
- 2 tsp paprika

Directions:

1. Mix all ingredients in a large saucepan and stir continuously over medium-low heat on cooking grid for 10 minutes, until desired consistency is obtained.
2. Store in refrigerator.

Simple Breadcrumbs

Prep Time: 10 minutes/ Cook Time 0 minute /
Serves: 4

Ingredients:

- 1 cup of almond flour/meal

- 1/2 a teaspoon of sea salt
- 1/2 a teaspoon of black pepper
- 1/2 a teaspoon of garlic powder
- 1/2 a teaspoon of dried parsley
- 1/4 teaspoon of onion powder
- 1/4 teaspoon of dried oregano

Directions:

1. Take a small-sized bowl and add all of the listed ingredients and whisk them well
2. Use as needed

Sour Cream

Prep Time: 10 minutes/ Cook Time 0 minute / Serves: 4

Ingredients:

- 1 can of thick unsweetened coconut milk
- 1 and a 1/2 tablespoon of lemon juice
- 1/2 a tablespoon of apple cider vinegar
- 1/8 teaspoon of salt

Directions:

1. Chill the coconut milk in the can overnight
2. Flip the can upside and open, pour off the liquid
3. Scrape out the thick cream and add lemon juice, salt, and vinegar
4. Whisk until smooth
5. Use it when needed!

Home-Made Mayonnaise

Prep Time: 10 minutes/ Cook Time 0 minute / Serves: 4

Ingredients:

- 1 whole egg
- 1/2 a teaspoon of sea salt
- 1/2 a teaspoon of ground mustard
- 1 and a 1/4 cup of extra light olive oil

- 1 tablespoon of lemon juice

Directions:

1. Place the egg, ground mustard, salt and 1/4 cup of olive oil into a food processor
2. Whirl on low until mixed
3. While the processor is running, drizzle remaining olive oil and keep whirling for 3 minutes
4. Add lemon juice and pulse on low until fully mixed
5. Chill for 30 minutes
6. Use as needed

Home-Made Tomato Sauce/Ketchup

Prep Time: 10 minutes/ Cook Time 0 minute / Serves: 4

Ingredients:

- 1/2 a cup of chopped pitted dates
- 1 can of 6-ounce tomato paste
- 1 can of 14 ounce diced tomatoes
- tablespoon of coconut vinegar
- 1/2 a cup of bone broth
- 1 teaspoon of garlic powder
- 1 teaspoon of onion powder
- 1 teaspoon of salt
- 1/2 a teaspoon of cayenne pepper

Directions:

1. Add the ingredients to a small-sized saucepan
2. Cook on medium-low for 20 minutes
3. Remove the heat
4. Take an immersion blender and blend the mixture until smooth
5. Remove the blender and simmer on low for 10 minutes
6. Use as needed

Cool Worcestershire Sauce

Prep Time: 10 minutes/ Cook Time 15 minute / Serves: 4

Ingredients:

- 1/2 a cup of apple cider vinegar
- tablespoon of water
- tablespoon of coconut aminos
- 1/4 teaspoon of mustard seeds
- 1/4 teaspoon of onion powder
- 1/4 teaspoon of garlic powder
- 1/8 teaspoon of cinnamon
- 1/8 teaspoon of black pepper

Directions:

1. Add all of the listed ingredients to your saucepan
2. Bring it to a boil and stir well
3. Simmer for a few minutes
4. Remove the heat and allow it to cool
5. Use as needed!

BBQ Sauce

Prep Time: 10 minutes/ Cook Time 15 minute / Serves: 4

Ingredients:

- 1/2 a cup of apple cider vinegar
- tablespoon of water
- tablespoon of coconut aminos
- 1/4 teaspoon of mustard seeds
- 1/4 teaspoon of onion powder
- 1/4 teaspoon of garlic powder
- 1/8 teaspoon of cinnamon
- 1/8 teaspoon of black pepper

Directions:

1. Add all of the listed ingredients to your saucepan
2. Bring it to a boil and stir well
3. Simmer for a few minutes
4. Remove the heat and allow it to cool
5. Use as needed!

Exciting Taco Seasoning

Prep Time: 10 minutes/ Cook Time 15 minute / Serves: 4

Ingredients:

- 1 tablespoon of Chili powder
- 1/2 a teaspoon of Garlic powder
- 1/2 a teaspoon of Onion powder
- 1 and a 1/2 teaspoon of ground cumin
- 1 teaspoon of salt
- 1 teaspoon of pepper
- 1/4 teaspoon of crushed red pepper flakes
- 1/4 teaspoon of dried oregano
- 1/2 a teaspoon of paprika

Directions:

1. Mix the above-mentioned ingredients to prepare the Taco seasoning and use it as needed.

Homely Fajita Seasoning

Prep Time: 10 minutes/ Cook Time 0 minute / Serves: 4

Ingredients:

- 1/4 cup of chili powder
- tablespoon of ground cumin
- 1 tablespoon of salt
- teaspoons of black pepper
- teaspoons of dried oregano
- teaspoons of paprika
- 1 teaspoon of onion powder
- 1 teaspoon of parsley

Directions:

1. Mix the above-mentioned ingredients to prepare the Taco seasoning and use it as needed.

The Brave Viking MIx

Prep Time: 10 minutes/ Cook Time 0 minute /

Serves: 4

Ingredients:

- teaspoons paprika
- teaspoons salt
- teaspoons onion powder
- 1 teaspoon cayenne
- 2 teaspoons ground pepper
- 1 teaspoon dry mustard

Directions:

1. Mix the above-mentioned ingredients to prepare the mix and use as needed

The Rosemary And Garlic Rub

Prep Time: 10 minutes/ Cook Time 0 minute / Serves: 4

Ingredients:

- 1 tablespoon pepper
- 1 tablespoon salt
- tablespoons fresh rosemary, chopped
- 1 tablespoon dried rosemary
- 8 garlic cloves, diced
- 1/2 cup olive oil

Directions:

1. Mix the above-mentioned ingredients to prepare the seasoning and use it as needed.

BBQ Beef Rub

Prep Time: 10 minutes/ Cook Time 0 minute / Serves: 4

Ingredients:

- 1 teaspoon salt
- 1/8 teaspoon ground cumin
- 3/4 teaspoon ground white pepper
- 3/4 teaspoon ground black pepper
- 3/4 teaspoon dried thyme
- 3/4 teaspoon ground savory
- 3/4 teaspoon ground coriander seeds
- 1 teaspoon ground bay leaves

- 1 and 1/2 teaspoon dried basil
- teaspoons garlic powder

Directions:

1. Mix the above-mentioned ingredients to prepare the seasoning and use as needed

Nutrition value per serving:

Calories: 11 kcal, Protein: 0.3 g, Fat: 0 g, Fiber: 0 g.

Herby Mixed Salt

Prep Time: 10 minutes/ Cook Time 0 minute / Serves: 4

Ingredients:

- 1/2 cup coarse salt
- 1/4 cup packed fresh rosemary leaves
- 1/4 cup packed fresh lemon thyme
- 1 cup of salt

Directions:

1. Mix the above-mentioned ingredients
2. Let it sit and Air Dry for 2 hours
3. Use as needed

Homely Fajita Seasoning

Prep Time: 10 minutes/ Cook Time 0 minute / Serves: 4

Ingredients:

- 1/4 cup of chili powder
- tablespoon of ground cumin
- 1 tablespoon of salt
- teaspoons of black pepper
- teaspoons of dried oregano
- teaspoons of paprika
- 1 teaspoon of onion powder
- 1 teaspoon of parsley

Directions:

1. Mix the above-mentioned ingredients to prepare the Taco seasoning and use it as

needed.

Nutrition value per serving:

Calories: 100 kcal, Protein: 0 g, Fat: 0 g, Fiber: 0 g.

Uncle Johnny's Premium Rub

Prep Time: 10 minutes/ Cook Time 0 minute / Serves: 4

Ingredients:

- 1/2 teaspoon oregano
- tablespoons ground paprika
- 1 tablespoon brown sugar
- 1 tablespoon ground cumin
- 1 tablespoon chili powder
- 1 tablespoon mustard powder
- 1 tablespoon salt
- tablespoons pepper
- 1 tablespoon garlic powder

Directions:

1. Mix the above-mentioned ingredients to prepare the seasoning and use it as needed.

The Greek Spice Rub

Prep Time: 10 minutes/ Cook Time 0 minute / Serves: 4

Ingredients:

- 1 teaspoon dried thyme
- 1 teaspoon dried parsley
- teaspoons dried oregano
- 1/2 teaspoon dried marjoram
- 1/2 teaspoon ground nutmeg
- 1/2 teaspoon ground cinnamon
- 1 teaspoon chicken bouillon granules
- 1 and 1/2 teaspoons garlic powder
- 1 teaspoon cracked pepper
- 1/2 teaspoon salt
- 1 and 1/2 teaspoon onion powder

Directions:

1. Mix the above-mentioned ingredients to prepare the seasoning and use it as needed.

Chapter 13: Game Recipes

Wild Elk Tenderloin Kabobs

Prep time: 15 minutes, Cook time: 15 minutes; Serves 8-10

Ingredients

- 3 lb elk tenderloin, cut into 2-inch chunks
- 3 tbsp balsamic vinegar
- 3 tbsp olive oil
- 3 yellow squash, whole
- 3 zucchini, whole
- 12 sweet peppers, small
- 12 cherry tomatoes
- 2 tbsp Traeger prime rib rub

Preparation Method

1. Drizzle elk tenderloin chunks with vinegar and oil then let sit in a bowl, large.
2. Meanwhile, chop squash and zucchini into 3/4 -inch thick coins.
3. Now cut ends off from the peppers and remove seeds.
4. Place peppers, tomatoes, zucchini, and squash coins to the bowl with tenderloin then toss them. Add more vinegar and oil until everything is lightly coated. Now generously add rib rub and continue tossing.
5. Stack meat and vegetables alternating them onto a skewer. This will make a kabob, perfect looking.
6. In the meantime, preheat your Grill to 500°F with the lid closed for about 15 minutes.
7. Place the kabobs on the grate directly and grill for about 15 minutes.

8. Remove from the Grill and enjoy it.

Smoked Spatchcocked Cornish Game Hens

Prep time: 25 minutes, Cook time: 45 minutes; Serves 2-4

Ingredients

- 4 Cornish game hens
- 2 oz Traeger big game rub

Preparation Method

1. Place the hens on a cutting board with breast side down and cut from neck to tailbone with poultry shears. This is to get rid of the backbone and help you see the bird inside.
2. Make a slit in the hen's cartilage at the breastbone base. This is to reveal the keel bone.
3. Now open the bird like a book while holding the ribs with both hands and facing down on your cutting board. Remove keel bone and cut slits behind the bird's legs.
4. Tuck drumsticks into the legs to hold them together.
5. Meanwhile, season the birds on both sides using the rub.
6. Preheat your Grill to 275°F with the lid closed for about 15 minutes.
7. Now, place the hens with skin side up on the Grill.
8. Cook for about 45 minutes until the internal temperature reads 160°F.
9. Transfer into a cutting board and rest for about 10 minutes.

10. Serve and enjoy.

Smoked Venison Tenderloin

Prep time: 5 minutes, Cook time: 2 hours; Serves 4

Ingredients

- 1 lb venison tenderloin
- 1/4 cup lemon juice
- 1/4 cup olive oil
- 5 garlic cloves
- 1 tbsp salt
- 1 tbsp black pepper, ground + more for serving

Preparation Method

1. Place venison tenderloins in a large bowl.
2. Process all the other ingredients in a blender until broken into small pieces and all is incorporated.
3. Pour and massage the marinade over the venison and refrigerate it for about 4 hours or overnight.
4. Now remove venison tenderloins from the marinade, rinse, pat dry, and cool at room temperature for about 30 minutes.
5. Preheat your Grill to 275°F.
6. Place the venison on to your Grill and smoke for about 2 hours until nice and juicy. Make sure internal temperature reads 130°F to 140°F for rare and medium-rare respectively.
7. Slice and top with more pepper then Remove and rest for about 10 minutes.
8. Enjoy!

Grilled Quail, South Carolina Style

Prep time: 20 minutes, Cook time: 20 minutes, Serves 4

Ingredients

- 4 tbsp butter
- 1/2 grated onion
- 3-4 tbsp vegetable oil
- 1/2 cup yellow mustard
- 1/2 cup sugar, brown
- 1/2 cup cider vinegar
- 1 tbsp dry mustard
- 1 tbsp cayenne
- Salt to taste
- 8-16 quails

Preparation Method

1. Heat butter over high-medium heat then sauté onions for about 3-4 minutes until translucent.
2. Add all other ingredients except quails and simmer for about 20 minutes. Simmer slowly.
3. Buzz in a blender to make a smooth sauce.
4. Flatten and remove quails backbone by cutting along the side using kitchen shears. Place the quails on a cutting board with breast side up then press them to flatten.
5. Meanwhile, preheat your Grill to high heat then place then lay your quails with breast side up.
6. Grill the quails with the lid closed for about 5 minutes. Rub the breast side using your sauce as it cooks.
7. Turn over the quails and grill for another 2 minutes with the lid open.
8. Turn over again and rub with sauce once more, cover your Grill and cook for another 2-4 minutes.
9. Remove quails from the Grill and rub with sauce once more.
10. Serve and enjoy.

Grilled Rabbit

Prep time: 5 minutes, Cook time: 40 minutes; Serves 8

Ingredients

- 1 whole rabbit fryer
- 1 cup spicy plum sauce
- **For grilling:** assorted veggies

Preparation Method

1. Preheat your Grill to medium-high.
2. In the meantime, cut your rabbit rib cage pressing down flat.
3. Spread half of the sauce on the rabbit inside then lay the rabbit on the Grill with marinade side down.
4. Now turn heat to low, 425°F, and cover. Cook for about 15-20 minutes.
5. After 15-20 minutes coat the rabbit top side with the remaining sauce and flip the rabbit long ways then coat using last of your sauce.
6. Add assorted veggies and cover the Grill. Cook for an additional 15-20 minutes until internal temperature reads 160°F and all juices run clear.
7. Remove and rest for about 10 minutes.
8. Chop into 8 chunks.
9. Serve and enjoy.

Smoked Doves

Prep time: 30 minutes, Cook time: 2 hours; Serves 10

Ingredients

- 1/2 cup kosher salt
- 2 quarts water
- 16-20 doves
- **Optional:** 1 tbsp instacure no.1

For guajillo sauce

- 5 unpeeled garlic cloves
- 1 quartered white onion, small and roughly chopped
- 2-5 hot chiles
- 8 guajillo peppers, dried and stems/seeds removed
- 2 tbsp tomato paste
- 1 tbsp Mexican oregano, dried
- 1/4 tbsp allspice
- 1/4 tbsp coriander, ground
- Salt to taste
- Lime juice to taste

Preparation Method

1. Dissolve salt in water then submerge the doves in the water. Refrigerate for about 4 hours. Now remove from the fridge, rinse and pat them dry.
2. Preheat your Grill to 170°F-200°F.
3. Place the doves on the Grill and smoke for about 2 hours.
4. In the meantime, rehydrate chiles by pouring boiling water over.
5. Char garlic and onions in a dry skillet, hot, until nice blackening. Now peel the garlic and place both onions and garlic in a blender.
6. Add chiles and remaining sauce ingredients into your blender. Process until smooth while adjusting seasoning with lime juice and salt. You can add water to thin the sauce.
7. Remove the doves from the Grill, half them using kitchen shears and coat with the sauce.
8. Serve and enjoy with napkins and bone bowl.

Smoked Pheasant

Prep time: 15 minutes, Cook time: 1 hour; serves 2-4

Ingredients

- 3 whole pheasant
- 3 tbsp smoky okie's rooster booster rub
- 1 quartered red bell pepper, whole, and core removed
- 1 white onion, whole and sliced to thin

sections
- 4 tbsp olive oil
- Pepper to taste
- Salt to taste
- 1 whole box rice pilaf, Uncle Ben's

Preparation Method

1. Preheat your Grill to 275°F while lid closed for about 10-15 minutes.
2. Clean pheasant thighs and breasts then rinse and place in a zip lock bag, large. Add rooster booster rub and a generous amount of Grill Saskatchewan rub shaking vigorously. Set aside.
3. Brush pepper and onions lightly using oil then splash with pepper and salt. Place them on a tin foil and to one side of your grill.
4. Smoke the veggies for about 1 hour then place your pheasant on the grill.
5. Cook for about 30-45 minutes.
6. Now remove everything from the grill.
7. Serve with rice pilaf.
8. Enjoy!

Smoked Guinea fowl with cranberry/orange glaze

Prep time: 5 minutes, Cook time: 1 hour 45 minutes; Serves 6

Ingredients

- 1 guinea fowl

For the rub
- 3 tbsp salt
- 1 tbsp pepper
- 2 tbsp ginger powder
- 2 tbsp cinnamon powder
- 2 tbsp oregano, dried

Cranberry-orange glaze
- 2 cups chicken broth
- 1 orange juice
- 2/3 cup cranberry jam

- A pinch of cinnamon powder
- A pinch of ginger powder

Preparation Method

1. Mix all the sauce ingredients in a medium saucepan and boil.
2. Lower heat and cook gently until sauce reduces having a syrup texture.
3. Meanwhile, mix all rub ingredients using your hands breaking up any clumps.
4. Search a hole on the guinea fowl neck. This is to slice your finger underneath the guinea fowl skin. Now separate meat from the skin and apply rub between the skin and the meat.
5. Poke holes with a sharp knife in the sin and rub its abdominal cavity.
6. Refrigerate the guinea fowl for a few hours.
7. In the meantime, preheat your Grill to 250°F.
8. Smoke your guinea fowl until internal temperature reads 50°C.
9. Turn heat to 845°F then splash guinea fowl with sunflower oil. This is to crisp skin.
10. Bake until golden brown tint on the skin and internal temperature reads 65°C.
11. Apply a thin glaze layer on the guinea fowl just a few minutes before internal temperate is reached.
12. Grill until glaze sticks on the skins and slightly caramelize the skin.
13. Enjoy!

Smoked Moose Roast with Cranberry-Mint Sauce

Prep time: 2 hours, Cook time: 1 hour 15 minutes; Serves 6

Ingredients

- 2-1/2 lbs moose loin roast

- Salt to taste, kosher
- 2 tbsp olive oil
- Favorite rub
- 1 can, 14-oz, cranberry sauce, whole berry
- 1/4 tbsp cardamom, ground
- 1 tbsp chopped mint, fresh and packed
- Cracked pepper to taste, fresh

Preparation Method

1. Tie moose roast using kitchen wire and season with salt then let it sit for 2 hours at room temperature. Once 2 hours are over, pat dry using paper towels.
2. Preheat a Grill to 275°F.
3. Meanwhile, heat oil over high-medium heat in a pan until oil starts to smoke. Now sear your meat until a golden crust on all sides.
4. Remove meat from the pan and splash with rub generously.
5. Smoke the meat in your Grill for about 1 hour until internal temperature reads 125°F.
6. Remove meat and loosely wrap in foil then allow your meat to carry over until 135°F for medium-rare.
7. In the meantime, combine cranberry sauce, cardamom, mint, pepper, and salt. Heat on low occasionally stirring until warmed through.
8. Once the meat has rested for about 10-15 minutes, slice the meat against the grain.
9. Serve with cranberry-mint sauce.
10. Enjoy with sides of choice.

Grilled Ultimate Game Burger

Prep time: 10 minutes, Cook time: 15 minutes; Serves 2-4

Ingredients

- 3/4 lb. wild boar, ground
- 3/4 lb. venison, ground
- Pepper to taste
- Salt to taste
- 2 tbsp. mayonnaise
- 1 tbsp. ketchup
- 2 tbsp. sweet pickle relish
- 1/2 tbsp. sugar
- 1/2 tbsp. white vinegar
- 1 sliced white onion
- 4 buns
- 4 American cheese pieces
- 4 lettuce pieces
- 1 sliced tomato

Preparation Method

1. Place and combine venison and boar in a bowl, mixing. Do not overwork.
2. Form 4, 1/3 lb. patties, from the meat mixture and generously splash with pepper and salt.
3. Mix all sauce ingredients in a bowl and set aside.
4. Start your Grill on smoke for about 4-5 minutes with the lid open until fire establishes.
5. Preheat the Grill to 400°F while lid closed for about 10-15 minutes.
6. Now arrange the patties on the Grill grate.
7. Cook until the desired doneness and until internal temperature reaches 160°F. Flip once.
8. Place the sliced onion on the grill 5 minutes before cooking is over.
9. During the last minutes, place cheese on your burgers and your buns on the grill.
10. Remove and build the burgers with a burger patty, bun, lettuce, tomato, and the grilled onions.
11. Enjoy!

Smoked Venison Loin

Prep Time: 20 minutes/ Cook Time 30 minutes / Serves: 4

Ingredients:

- 1 and 1/4 pounds loin of venison
- Salt to taste
- Pinch of ground cumin
- 4 tablespoons almond oil
- 1 shallot, chopped
- 1 garlic clove, peeled
- 1 teaspoon pink peppercorn
- 1 teaspoon sesame seeds
- 4 courgettes, sliced
- 3 fresh lemons

Directions:

1. Season venison with salt and pepper
2. Pre-heat your Grill to 300 degrees F and set it for direct cooking
3. Roast venison on the grid, making sure to keep turning it for every 60-90 seconds, cook for 5-7 minutes
4. Take a pan and add oil, shallots, garlic, pink peppercorn, sesame seeds and heat for 30 seconds
5. Add courgettes and cook for 2 minutes on high heat
6. Drizzle lemon juice on top and serve with venison

The Big Game Hen

Prep Time: 10 minutes/ Cook Time 2-3 hours / Serves: 4

Ingredients:

- 2 Cornish game hens
- Salt as needed
- Freshly ground black pepper
- 4 tablespoon of butter
- 1 cup of quick-cooking seasoned brown rice
- 1 small coarsely chopped small onion
- 1/2 a cup of squeezed orange juice
- 1/2 a cup of apricot jelly

Directions:

1. Season the birds with salt and pepper
2. Take a small saucepan over low heat and add 2 tablespoons of butter, melt the butter and stir in rice and onion
3. Stuff the hens with the rice mix and secure the legs with twine
4. Rinse the saucepan and put it back to low heat
5. Melt remaining 2 tablespoons of butter and stir in orange juice alongside apricot jelly
6. Whisk until smooth
7. Baste the hen with the jelly glaze
8. Pre-heat your Grill to 275 degrees F and set it for in-direct cooking
9. Transfer to Grill and smoke for 2-3 hours until internal temperature reaches 170 degrees F
10. Brush with more jelly and enjoy it!

The Big Goose Breast

Prep Time: 10 minutes/ Cook Time 6 hours / Serves: 4

Ingredients:

- 1/2 a cup of orange juice
- 1/3 cup of olive oil
- 1/3 cup of Dijon mustard
- 1/3 cup of brown sugar
- 1/4 cup of soy sauce
- 1/4 cup of honey
- 1 tablespoon of dried minced onion
- 1 teaspoon of garlic powder
- 8 goose breast halves

Directions:

1. Take a medium-sized bowl and a whisk in orange juice, olive oil, mustard, soy sauce, sugar, honey, onion, garlic powder
2. Mix well and prepare the marinade
3. Transfer the goose breast to the marinade and cover
4. Allow it to refrigerate for 3-6 hours
5. Heat your Grill to 300 degrees Fahrenheit
6. Transfer the breast to your Grill grate and brush smoke for 6 hours, making sure to keep brushing it with the marinade for the first 30 minutes
7. Keep smoking until the internal temperature reaches 165 degrees Fahrenheit
8. Serve and enjoy!

Herbed Quail Dish

Prep Time: 20 minutes/ Cook Time 60 minutes / Serves: 4

Ingredients:

- 4-6 quail
- 2 tablespoon of olive oil
- Salt as needed
- Freshly ground black pepper
- 1 pack of dry Hidden Valley Ranch dressing (or your preferred one)
- 1/2 a cup of melted butter

Directions:

1. Pre-heat your Grill to 225 degrees Fahrenheit
2. Brush the quail with olive oil and season with salt and pepper Place the in your Grill and smoke for 1 hour
3. Take a small bowl and add ranch dressing mix and melted butter
4. After the first 30 minutes of smoking, brush the quail with the ranch mix Repeat at the end of the cooking time
5. Once the internal temperature of the quail reaches 145 degrees Fahrenheit, they are ready!

Honey Game Turkey

Prep Time: 20 minutes/ Cook Time 6 hours / Serves: 4

Ingredients:

- 1 gallon of hot water
- 1 pound of kosher salt
- 2 quarts of vegetable broth
- 8-ounce jars of honey
- 1 cup of orange juice
- A 7-pound bag of ice cubes
- pound of the whole turkey with giblets and neck removed
- 1/4 cup of vegetable oil
- 1 teaspoon of poultry seasoning
- 1 granny smith apples cored and cut up into large chunks
- 1 celery stalk cut up into small chunks
- 1 small sized onion cut up into chunks
- 1 quartered orange

Directions:

1. Take a 54-quart cooler and add kosher salt and hot water
2. Mix them well until everything dissolves
3. Add vegetable broth, orange juice, and honey
4. Pour ice cubes into the mix and add the turkey into your brine, keeping the breast side up
5. Lock up the lid of your cooler and let it marinate overnight for 12 hours
6. Make sure that the brine temperature stays under 40 degree Fahrenheit
7. Remove the turkey from the brine and

discard the brine
8. Dry the turkey using a kitchen towel
9. Take a bowl and mix vegetable oil and poultry seasoning
10. Rub the turkey with the mixture
11. Place apple, onion, celery and orange pieces inside the cavity of the turkey
12. Pre-heat your Grill to a temperature of 400 degrees Fahrenheit
13. Set your turkey onto your Grill and insert a probe into the thickest part of your turkey breast
14. Set the probe for 160 degrees Fahrenheit
15. Smoke the turkey for 2 hours until the skin is golden brown
16. Cover the breast, wings, and legs using aluminum foil and keep smoking it for 2-3 hours until the probe thermometer reads 160 degrees Fahrenheit
17. Make sure to keep adding some hickory chips to your heat box occasionally
18. Remove the vegetables and fruit from the cavity of your Turkey and cover it up with aluminum foil
19. Let it rest of 1 hour and carve it up!

Conclusion

With so many deliciously unique recipes, your *Grill & Smoker* lifestyle is about to get interesting.

Good luck!